Drafts: 100 Letters I Will *Never* Send

Nkosilesisa Kwanele Ncube

Drafts: 100 Letters I Will *Never* Send

EAN 978-1-77925-978-3
ISBN 9781779259783

© Nkosilesisa Kwanele Ncube

Published in 2020

Edited by Fikile Nomadlozi Nyathi
Cover & Illustration by Mhle Nzima
Typeset by Kudzai Chikomo

Copyright Reserved

All rights reserved. No part of this publication may be reproduced, stored in a retrieval system or transmitted in any form or by any means, electronic, mechanical, photocopying, recording, or otherwise without prior permission of the author or publisher

Dedication

To my father Dr NJ Ncube who always wanted me to write a book and would have carried this everywhere.

Acknowledgements

I would like to thank the following people. Without whom this book would not have happened:

God: For the incredible guts that it took to put this together and the strength to see it through.

Family and friends who never ran out of insights to share. Your support will always be appreciated.

I have written you a long letter
because I did not have the time to write you a short one.
-Mark Twain

About the Author

Nkosilesisa, better known as Nkosi is a trained journalist, screenwriter and aspiring television producer whose interests lie in story telling through whatever medium. To date she has written full length and short form films and has also written for television. She also interned at the national weekly newspaper "Sunday News" for a year and had a short stint as editor for an online entertainment magazine "Urban Culxure". She is currently with the Multichoice Talent Factory where she is working towards improving her skills in film. In her spare time, Nkosi runs a personal blog www.wordsbynkocy.com. Her other skills include public speaking and concept development.

CONTENTS

FAMILY

11	To Dad (RIP)
12	To My Mother
14	To Grandma, Who I Don't Remember Well
16	To My Brother
17	To My Sister
19	To My Son
21	To My Daughter
23	To My Grandpa
24	To My Uncle (Replacement Dad)
25	To The Sister I Didn't Know I Had
27	To My Parents
29	To My Fave Cousin
30	To My Aunt (Replacement mum)
31	To Our Helper
32	To The Future Father of My child
34	To My Future In-Laws
35	To The Guy Who Marries My Sister
36	To The Girl Who Marries My Brother
37	To All The Dogs I have Loved Before
39	To Dad, Now That I think About It

FRIENDS

42	To My Best Friend
43	To My Girl Squad
44	To My Guy Squad
45	To My First Friend
46	To the friend Who Died Too Young
48	To The Friend I No Longer Speak To

50 To My Roommate
52 To My Best Male Friend
54 To The Friend I Hit Puberty With
55 To My Newly Married Friends

BOYS

57 To The One Who Would Have Been The One That Got Away
59 To The One Who Actually Got Away
61 To The Girl He Loved Before Me
62 To The One I Failed To Make It Work With- Twice
64 To The One I Broke
66 To The One
68 To The One Who Gets This Version Of Me
69 To The Girl He Chose Over Me
71 To My Most Consistent Booty Call
72 To My Crush
74 To The Entanglement
75 To the Girl We Cheated On
77 To The Wild Card
79 To Guys Leaving Me On Read

GOD

81 To God
83 To God, A Thank You Note.

PEOPLE

86 To You Dear Reader
87 To My Mentor
89 To My Favourite Teacher

90	To The Rest of The world
92	To The Men Staring As I Walk By
94	To Girls Worried About Fat and Folds
95	To The Guy Who Sexually Assaulted My Friend
97	To The Varsity Staff Member We Didn't Report
99	To User ZimboHotboi33 On Instagram
100	To Anyone Working Through Grief
102	To Girls Who Lost Their Daddies
104	To Anyone Who Lost Somebody To Suicide
106	To Anyone Dealing With Depression
107	To Body Shamers
109	To My Younger Self
111	To My Future Self
112	To Anyone Who Cares (In Case I Die)
114	To Girls Who Have Been Called Intimidating
116	To Black Girls
117	To The Struggling Artist
119	To The Public Income Kid In A Private School
121	To Drunk Girls In Bathrooms
123	To Anyone Asking When I'll Get Married.
124	To My President
125	To Ota Benga
127	To Chimamanda Ngozi Adichie
128	To Shonda Rhimes
130	To Naya Rivera
131	To Jada, You Were Wrong
133	To Amy Winehouse, P!NK and Halsey
134	To Blair Waldorf.
135	To Chuck Bass
136	To Beth and Randall Pearson
137	To Elena Gilbert
139	To Anyone Thinking of Writing A Book

A MILLION LITTLE THINGS

- 141 To My Period
- 142 To Tampons
- 143 To Privilege
- 145 To My Body
- 147 To My Eating Disorder
- 149 To My Anxiety
- 151 To My Inhaler
- 152 To My Glasses
- 153 To Chocolate and Cake
- 154 To The Gym
- 155 To My Size 32 Jeans
- 156 To The Hoodie I Refuse To Return
- 158 To Vodka
- 159 To My Bedroom
- 160 To Boarding School
- 161 To My University Degree
- 162 To The 5+ Years Missing From Zimbabwean History
- 164 To the Year 2019
- 165 To Covid 19

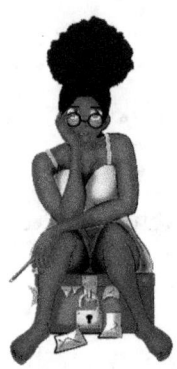

FAMILY

"Having somewhere to go is home.
Having someone to love is family.
And having both is a blessing."

To Dad (RIP)

I'm sorry.

I forgive you.

I love you.

To My Mother

Of all the letters I have written, I think this was the most complex. What do I say to you in one letter? How do I sum up everything in one document? What do you say to someone who gave you life then spent every waking moment since then giving to you and expecting nothing in return?

I want to say thank you but that seems a little insulting in the face of everything you have done for me. But no language has anything better than thank you. So let's go with that. Thank you for the countless times you have put my needs above yours. Even now as I am an adult (allegedly), you still do as much for me as you did when I was a child. Ngiyabonga MaNdlo.

Thank you for being my friend. I always think it's quite difficult to decide where you start being my friend and where you start being my mother. However, that is a line that you have walked very well for as long as I have known you. I believe your openness and your ability to talk to us as equals is part of the reason we (dare I say) turned out as well as we did.

I apologise for the many times I made you sad. My words aren't always the most thought out and sometimes they hurt and I cannot apologize enough for the times you fell victim to them. I'm sorry for the times I was unreasonably difficult or unreasonably selfish or just plain unreasonable. You deserved so much better than mood swings and attitude from a 14 year old girl.

You are one of the most resilient people I know. You survived a lot of things that should have broken you but you always managed to come out on the other side. And it's not just the coming out that I admire, it's the coming out smiling that does it for me. I suppose one of the most important things I have learnt from you is that there is nothing so ominous in this world that it can't be laughed at. I am in awe of your strength and your faith and if I have just a fraction of that someday then I know I will survive anything that life throws at me. I love you ma and I really hope you are proud of the person I became.

To Grandma, who I don't remember well

Mum posted a picture of you on Mothers' Day and it got me thinking. I remember you, but they are not vivid memories. I mean they are not even elaborately great memories; they are just very normal memories. For one I remember us spending days together when everyone else was at school or work. I remember very vaguely one time you asking me what I had dreamt of the night before and I remember you trying to explain what death was and who Nkomo was in 1999 because everyone was talking about this Nkomo who I didn't know and you explained it to me.

I think this is where my memories of you begin and end and that's just a terrible place to be. I lived with you for an entire year and it sucks that this is all I get from the four years I knew you and the year I lived with you. I wish I had known you better. There is so much about you that I would have loved to know. I never know whether or not to bring you up to mum or grandpa because I don't know how talking about you makes them feel.

I will however say that whenever mum mentions you, there is this look on her face. I can never place it. It's a very tender look that I don't see all that often. And when she does talk about you, she says you had the best heart of anyone she knew. She says you were generous and she says you worked really hard. From what she says I gather you were quite the entrepreneur, of course nobody called it that back then but it's nice to know you were ahead of your time.

Thank you for the family you blessed me with. You gave me two mums who love me unconditionally, and your husband is still the best man I have ever known, all these years later. I just wish I would have been able to do for you what you did for me. And I wish I could remember you better because then I could be able to imagine what you would say about things or how you would feel about them. But I got what I got and I promise to hold that close to my heart.

Continue resting angel.

To My Brother

When we were kids, the one thing that always annoyed me about you was that you were always laughing at me. It didn't matter what I did, I just knew you would find a way to. But as we grow up, I have found that that is my favorite thing about you. You have the kind of sense of humour that trumps any mood, any cloud of gloom...you are the most hilarious person I know. But it's not just about laughs for you. I have always admired your maturity. How well you handle things that anybody would throw grenades with a calm that only you can conjure up. I really wish I could be like that.

I miss you. Sure we text but it's different. I miss having your room just down the corridor and knowing that you're always there. I miss the sound of your music echoing throughout the house from your room. I miss how excited you would get for New Years. It's the small things that matter.

The worst part about adulting is that your siblings don't get to be your roommates anymore and I suppose that creates room for us to grow. And grow you have. I always knew you were very resourceful but I'm thrown by how much you have grown. I am proud of everything you have accomplished and I am grateful that you have given me someone to look up to as well as be proud of.

I love you for always. X

To My Sister

You are my favourite person in the world. And I have met some really incredible people but you will always be top of that list. It's very easy for anyone to assume that you are my favourite person simply because you are my sister. But that is not the reason why. You are my favourite person because I like you. Under a lot of circumstances, love is considered to be bigger than like. However, when you are born into a family with somebody, love is never an option. You can't not love someone you have known your entire life. So I can't go to town about how much I love you, it was never a choice. I love you because we were born into the same family and I have known you my entire life. I like you because of the person you are.

I like you because you make me laugh more than anyone I have ever known. I like that I can make you laugh more than anyone else I know. I love our inside jokes that no one else would get even if they tried. I like that you know what I'm thinking before I say it; how one look with you replaces an entire conversation. I like how ready you always are to say what everybody else is thinking and I love that nothing I do is ever too much for you. Never too loud or too annoying or too over the top. I like that I know I always have your support. Someone said to us once that our relationship was so great because you, being older created an environment that permitted it. I like you for that.

I am very often in awe of you and while the petty side of me gets annoyed at you for giving me so much to live up to, the rest of me is so proud of the person you are constantly growing into. You are a major part of the reason I push myself as hard as I do, because you deserve a little sister who makes you as proud as you make her.

You deserve all the best things in life. You deserve love and laughter and you deserve to stand in the sun and dance it out. I love you. But more importantly, I will always like you.

To My Son

Baby Boy. For as long as I can remember, whenever I imagined myself as a mother, I always imagined myself mothering a girl or two. But you're here now. This is not to say you are not wanted. You are so wanted, so loved, so appreciated but mostly so unprepared for. See, here's the thing, mummy never got to see how baby boys are raised- your uncle was already halfway through adulthood when mummy started paying attention to these things. So most of my work with you is going to be experimental and for that I apologise.

I want you to learn early on that there is power in emotions. I know we live in a world that perceives any show of emotion from a man as weakness. I want you to rise above that, I want you to feel things, and speak out when you feel things. Because there are way too many men that keep things bottled inside until it is too late. I want you cry when you need to, there is no greater strength than that of owning your feelings. I want you to normalise it, it may be too late for the generations of men before you but you are where we fix that. Be sensitive that keeps you beautifully human.

Girls will come and girls will go. Respect each of them. Understand the concept of consent. I have to tell you this although I believe this has been said to you a lot of times but I will always feel better knowing that I told you, knowing that I taught you how it works. If a girl tells you no, then it's no, if a girl is drunk, that counts as a no. Don't catcall girls on the street, don't stare at girls, don't get mad at girls who reject you. You are not entitled to any girl's attention or phone number or body, it's a choice girls make- a gift if you may from her to you.

Don't rape. It sounds like an odd thing to have to say. It may even sound horrible coming from your mother because how could I ever think you would, right. But I also understand that every rapist, every woman basher under the sun is somebody's son and maybe if their mother or somebody else had told them not to, then maybe they would have turned out differently.

As a black boy from a minority ethnic group, I want you to know there may always be a target on your back. I have no explanation as to why this target exists, the least I can do is try to tell you how to steer clear of this target but even this is not fool proof. You may end up dead or beaten or tortured just because of the colour of your skin or because of the language that you speak and nothing scares me more than this. So I may tell you to obey the law, to respect agents of the law, to run away from conversations about race and ethnicity because God forbid you are too loud about these. The truth is nothing I tell you can prepare you for any of it and this breaks my heart.

That aside, I will love you with everything in me, I will attend everything you are a part of, I will cheer for you, I will cry and I will grow along with you. I love you.

To My Daughter

Dear Menenzia or Modester or Ambrosia or Prudence or...know what, when the time comes, I'll know what to call you.

Honey I could lie to you and say that this life thing is always going to be easy, and that you'll always have the answers and that you'll be everyone's favourite person all the time. That would be easy, right. But come on, you're my daughter and easy has never been your speed...you're going to be just like mummy, only better.

You'll roll your eyes and make a snide remark every ten seconds, you'll have trouble taking instructions and all too often, you'll blurt out the wrong thing. You'll talk too freely about your period, people will frown upon your crude jokes (because well brought up ladies don't joke like that, right) and you might find death jokes aren't as funny to everyone else as they are to you.

I want you to know from the onset that the universe belongs to you. Baby, the world is your stage and I want you to own it, and if anyone tries telling you the world doesn't revolve around you, tell them they're wrong because mummy says the world does revolve around you and mummy knows best.

They'll probably call you egotistical and selfish and entitled, the braver ones might even call you a bitch...but whatever, you deserve the world and anyone who has less than that to offer you really has no business being anywhere near you.

At 17, you'll discover boys; one boy in particular. He'll be a pastor's kid with a dark side and because you're my daughter, you'll be drawn to the irony and poetry that is his existence. For years after meeting each other, you'll break each other and tear each other down and still call it love. Ultimately, nothing will come out of it, but you'll be a much better person for the experience.

On your 19th birthday, you'll discover alcohol and that's ok, mama don't judge. Just don't come telling me about it, I'm still your mother. Somewhere along the way, you might want to discover what your body can do in relation to another person's body, boy or girl; mama still don't judge. I could go the typical route and tell you that sex gives away your power but...

Your power is not between your legs, so nothing that goes on there could take away or add to said power. Baby, your power is in your mind, it's in your thoughts, your reflections, the books that you read, the company that you keep, the prayers that you whisper...that's where your power lies.

You won't be everybody's cup of tea and I want you to know that that's ok; it's a special thing to be. You're going to be a handful-full of opinions and questions and tantrums and truth is...half the time, I won't know what to do with you, but I promise to do my best.

I can totally wait to meet you, no hurry.

To My Grandpa

One of my earliest memories is of me waking up in a hospital bed. I think I was three or four at the time and when I opened my eyes, you were sitting by my bedside, watching me. I don't know how many times I have thought of that moment. One thing that remains constant is how dependable you are. There has never been a time when we called you and you failed to show up. You are always present whether for something as serious as a death in the family or something as small as a leaking tap.

I suppose you are part of the reason why men generally underwhelm me. Having been loved by you and seeing the kind of man you are has made me quite impatient with anyone who is less than the man that you are. The downside of this becomes that everyone then somehow falls short. Should that be the price I have to pay for knowing you and being loved by you, I will gladly pay it.

I thank God for you everyday. Not only because you are my grandpa but also because you have been around for as long as you have been. I am grateful that you have watched me grow to a point where I can slowly start to repay you for the countless things you have done. Not that I ever could repay you because your impact in my life is not something I can put a tag to.

I think you pray harder for me than I pray for myself and I will always be grateful for that. Your prayers have gotten me into rooms I never could have dreamed of entering and kept me in spaces I didn't even think I deserved to be in in the first place. I pray the Lord gives you more years. You still have so much love and wisdom to give and we still have so much we need to do for you.

For always being there, I love you.

To My Uncle (Replacement Dad)

I am sorry I project so much of my loss onto you. You lost your brother and maybe it's unfair of me to lean on you as much as I do but I don't know what else to do. You are a lot like him in so many ways and whenever I spend time with you, I feel like he's back here with me. And I know how selfish it is of me to expect you to fill out every gap that he has left but I suppose it is part of my process. I suppose it's because you knew him longer than any of us did.

So let me reintroduce myself to you, as the daughter you didn't sign up for but you got anyway. I fuss about birthdays; they're a big deal to me. I now just need to learn yours off by heart and I swear I will overwhelm you with birthday messages so long, you will probably get tired before you read them to the end. I will fuss less about Fathers' Day, your boys get to keep that one.

I will think of the tiniest excuse to text you, I will think of reasons to see you any chance I get. I will hug you. There will be a lot of hugs, but don't worry I will ease you into it. Meanwhile thank you. Thank you for being here when he wasn't. Thank you for standing up for us when nobody else did. Thank you for being patient with me while I try to figure out how to go about our relationship.

See, it has been a while since I have been fathered and I don't quite remember how to go about it. All I know is you are here and I am too. And I will be here on good days and bad ones, I will be here sharing good news and I will be here crying over the bad things. I may also be here one day with a boy who will say things to you about marrying me, please be nice. Point is we're both here. Me having forgotten to be fathered and you never having to father a daughter, let's do this.

To The Sister I Didn't Know I Had

I don't do well with surprises. As you get to know me, you will realize that I am too much of a control freak to appreciate them. I like structure and routine and I like knowing what's going to happen. I am safer in spaces where I know what will happen. So you will understand why it took me a minute to get my head around your existence. It's not a personal attack on you as an individual. It's the situation.

I knew about you for four years before I made an effort to contact you. It was four years of me talking myself into being a bigger person and teaching myself how to handle you and my relationship with you. I wanted to be able to come correct to you. I didn't want to be the cliché evil step sister so I wanted to sort myself out before I let myself get to know you. I needed to move past any sense of betrayal or hurt or resentment before knowing you. I needed to remind myself that like me, you were just a kid who did nothing to contribute to the situation. You were dragged into it as much as I was.

And then I met you. I must admit, I was skeptical. What would I say to you? Would I like you? Would you like me? I'll admit I was under so much pressure that day. To prove that I was raised right and I was a good kid. But you were so kind and so warm and so accepting and all my pressure went away. I just decided to be me. To be your big sister.

Big sister. That is something I have never thought myself to be. See I have always been the baby. I'm the baby at home, I'm usually the youngest around my friends, I'm one of the youngest around cousins. I have no idea how to be a big sister. I have been taken care of my entire life and I have no idea what is expected of me in this regard. So please be patient with me as I learn how to do right by you.

I will mess it up along the way because that is the only way I know how to do anything. But I promise, as long as you give the opportunity to, I will always try. My abrasiveness will tiptoe around your sensibilities, my pessimism will stand down when you want to bask in the glory of optimism and when you do well at anything, I will clap and I will celebrate because that's what big sisters do.

To My Parents

I think a lot about how I don't give you enough credit for parenting us the way that you did. Mostly because I thought this was the standard model of parenting. I legitimately thought everybody was raised the same way that I was but as I get older, I realise how much you guys put into us turning out the way we did.

I appreciate how you taught us how to have difficult conversations very early in life. I remember watching 911 footage on CNN with mum. I was 6 at the time and Stu was 9 and I remember mum explaining what was going on; you didn't try to downplay it or talk down at us about it. You told us the truth. And a few years later, I remember us watching Saddam Hussein's execution as a family. I'm glad that we were the kind of family that watched the news together and shared opinions. By the time I was 7, I think I had a pretty fair appreciation of the world. I understood that although the world was great, it was also full of as much bad as it was of good. I never walked around with a false sense of how the world worked.

Thank you for teaching me the value of money. I remember earning my pocket money. I remember having to do crossword puzzles to earn 10 dollars. That taught me never to get comfortable with money that I hadn't earned. A lesson I wish a lot of girls my age had learnt when I did. You taught me to work for everything I have. I also remember whenever Paps would give me money, he would tell me to buy something tangible with it before spending it on temporary things. Mostly I am grateful that although we were comfortable, I always knew that whatever you had was yours, I was not entitled to it. If I wanted my own stuff, I would have to earn it.

You created an environment that enabled me to have a voice. It's only now that I realise that not every family calls a meeting before a big decision is made. I remember how meetings were called to discuss big purchases like vehicles and land. And I remember Stu having the responsibility of taking down minutes and Paps going around the room to ask people's opinions. You may not know this but this is where I learnt that I had a voice. That it didn't matter if I was the youngest person in the room or the least experienced, but if I had an opinion, I had to vocalise it. I don't think I would have gotten to where I am if I had not been encouraged to speak out from an early age.

I learnt equality at home. I'm glad you made a home where there were no boys and no girls; there were just children. We all did dishes, we all cleaned up dog poo, we all cleaned the car, we all jump started said car when it needed to be jump started. I will also always be grateful that you exposed us to as many different sides of life as you could. I went to a private preschool, a government primary school, a Catholic second primary school, a Presbyterian secondary school, a private high school and a State university. Because of this, there is not a single room that I could walk into and feel out of place.

Lastly, thank you letting me know that it was okay to fail. In all the trouble we ever got into, none of it was because we had failed at anything. I remember giving up on my driver's licence and getting pep talks from both of you about how human it was to fail. And every time I failed, you would both just say, "you will get it next time" and eventually I did. I don't think I would have if you two hadn't had my back then.

I suppose the irony of having educators for parents is that they will always find a way to teach. And that's what you guys did. You taught me how to be a person- a whole feeling, reacting and thinking person. I do not take that for granted.

To My Fave Cousin

I wish we had been this close earlier on. I know we were cool as kids but then there are a couple of years when we weren't really in touch. Those are the years I wish we had spent together. We have reconnected now and I am so glad we found each other.

You are one of my favourite people in the universe because you get me in ways that most people don't. You have been present for some of my worst decisions, my greatest memories, my lowest moments and you have been consistent in your love and support. You know everything there is to know about me and while your reactions to my shenanigans have been many, judgement has never been one of them. I appreciate that. You are also my go to person for a lot of things and I know I can always count on you.

What I love most about you is that even if we weren't related, I do not doubt that we would have made the best of friends. I can't wait to see how the rest of your life plays out. I can't wait to see you at the height of your career, as a dad, as a husband. But I'm not worried at all. I just know you will do amazing at these the way you do at everything else.

I have love for you always.

To My Aunt (Replacement mum)

You are such an inspiration. You are one of the strongest people I know. I have seen you weather giant storms with a smile on your face and with as much love in your heart as you ever have. I admire that.

I admire how you love life, how you are ready to dive head first into new situations because I suppose you understand better than most that it is so much better to regret having done something than to regret never having done it. May you never lose your zest for life, your wonder and your sense of adventure.

I love you and although we don't talk very often, I have never doubted the love that you have for me. I always feel your support from thousands of miles away. I have felt your love every time you have put your life on hold to try and help where I need it.

I know I don't say this enough: I love you to the ends of the world.

To Our Helper

I just spent a week without you and it made me realize how much my life depends on you and your competence. There are a million things that I take for granted because I never fully realize that they only happen because of the work that you put in. This week has shown me just how much you do for us!

I do not take any of it for granted. For ten years you have carried our day to day runnings on your back and perhaps we don't thank you enough. But as I walk into every clean room and sit down to a hot meal or put on a clean sweater, I am reminded of the work that you put in.

You have become like family over the years and I really hope you feel like we are your family too. Over the years, you have stood by and supported us through long nights and successes and lows and new jobs and funerals and the million little things that you do every day that we usually don't notice.

Above all, I appreciate that you sacrifice time with your own family to take care of ours. It is not a small thing you are doing and if ever you feel my gratitude does not extend the way it should. Please refer to this letter.

Gratitude and respect.

To The Future Father of My child

Oh lookie, we've made a human being.

And from now on, I suppose everything that we do, every choice that we make should lead up to the overall good of this tiny person.

In spite of ourselves, may we raise this child to be the best possible human being. To be kind, to treat people with respect, regardless of where they are from. May we afford our child opportunities, let them know that the world is theirs for the taking, let them know that whatever path they choose, they will always be unconditionally and unapologetically loved. May our child know love, appreciate what it is to love, appreciate what it is to be loved and may they turn out better than either of us thought they would.

May this child be the best of us! May our most Godly traits shine through this child. Whatever our shortcomings may be, as individuals and as a unit, may they never reflect as our failures as parents. In spite of what may or may not happen between us, may we never put this precious little being in a position where they have to choose between us because they deserve to have both of us in their lives. May we not foster any form of resentment on our child.

May we be so wise as to keep our prejudices from limiting who baby becomes. May we not project our experiences, our fears, our beliefs, our superstitions onto Baby. May we be brave enough to let our child find their own voice in the world, and decide who they want to be, without us ever imposing what we feel is right. May we keep the reins loose enough to let Baby explore the world but tight enough that should Baby need us, we are always there.

Let us surround our child with love, with laughter, with gifts, candy. Let us not take any differences that Baby has from us as an insult or as a rejection of our parenting. Let's learn tolerance now while we have the time and let's unlearn all our toxic tendencies because Baby deserves better. Let Baby know that baby is loved, by both mummy and daddy. Let baby be able to talk to mummy and daddy about anything.

Importantly, let's remember that we're stuck together for life. And that this requires understanding, kindness, suspending ego and a lot of compromise. We're partners before anything else. Let's do this right.

To My Future In-Laws

I can't start a fire for shit so let's negotiate.

First off, I am a human being not a birthing machine, not a washing machine not a cooking machine, none of that. I am a person who just happens to love your son or brother. Because I love him, I look forward to loving you too. My love for him may be unconditional but my relationship with you will need to be worked on.

You shall address me by my name. I am not *"malukazana"* or *"makoti"* or *"muroora"* or... *andizi lapho*, let's use names. My attendance of family gatherings will depend on how well we get along. Should there be any family drama, please keep me out of it; there will probably be enough of that where I come from. Micasa Sucasa but ultimately it is mi casa and while I will relish visits, I will not entertain visits that are either unannounced or last too long. I think boundaries are important.

You are going to be an important part of my children's lives so if for no other reason, then may we have a great relationship for the sake of the children. I want to surround them with love from both ends of the family so it matters to me that we get along.

It's a complex relationship we are trying to enter into. One family is hectic enough, having to take on a second family is going to take some hard work, some patience, tolerance and compromise. I am willing to do all of this if you in turn are willing to do the same.

Naturally, it won't always be smooth sailing but as long as intentions are kept pure, I promise to never stop trying.

To The Guy Who Marries My Sister

I will either be your best friend or the girl who fights you with hands. It all depends on how you treat her.

To The Girl Who Marries My Brother

You landed a good one.

And like I once said to my brother-in-law, I will either be your best friend or I will fight you.

Treat him right for the former.

To All The Dogs I have Loved Before

Dear Shumba, the first dog I ever interacted with. More than any other dog, you taught me that loyalty was earned. I remember how nobody other than your rightful owner i.e. my grandpa could feed you or bathe you or touch you. I love how you were so protective of us but at the same time reminding us that you weren't ours. You had one master and you would answer only to him. Rest in power king.

Dear Rasco -the first dog we had at our home. You were the gentlest, nicest gift anybody ever gave to us. You knew how to be a friend, you kept us company and you let me eat your dog biscuits, never once complaining. You were a friend, a pet, a guard, a babysitter. Thank you for showing me that we needed you as much as you needed us.

Dear Rambo, the second dog gifted to us. I never understood you bruh. You were a weird weird fellow. But now that I think about it, maybe you had never received love. Maybe you never knew what it was like to be part of a family, in a home. Thinking about it now, I should have tried harder to get to know you. I owed you that, I apologise. Above all, you taught me tolerance.

Ty. You will always have a special place in my heart. You were my first puppy and I had so many plans for you. I admit I went a little overboard but I swear I just wanted the best for you. It was through raising you that I learnt what it meant to be responsible for another life. So I fed you, bathed you, taught you to bark (I did say I went overboard), I grew up. Your death will always hit me the hardest because we saw it coming and we tried everything to keep you alive and it still didn't work. Love you always.

Fluffy, You adorable little ball of fur. You deserved a longer life than you got. You were by far the happiest dog I have ever had, hands down the naughtiest too. It is probably because you never got to grow into a full on dog. You would have been a joy to watch growing.

Lexie and Terry! Let me start with you Terry. I wish you had lived longer. I am sorry. Lexie, my darling - the only member of the sisterhood. I'm still gutted by how you left. Quietly, silently, no warning at all. But I suppose you died the way you lived. Peacefully and gracefully. Ever the doll, I'll miss how affectionate you were and how great you were at reading moods and how you always knew whether I wanted a quiet snuggle buddy or a playmate. Rest easy Queen.

Chubbs. As my sole surviving baby, I want you to know how loved you are. I'm just getting old baby. I know you feel ignored sometimes but I'm not as agile as I once was. To me you'll always be like that oops baby that one has at 60. I love you but there is no way I will be able to keep up with you. You have taught me patience. You have taught me how in the middle of busy schedules and deadlines and classes, I should always stop and breathe and slow dance with you. You are precious. You are loved.

To Dad, Now That I think About It

I read the last letter I wrote to you and while it was honest, it was a very cowardly letter to write. It said a lot without saying anything and then I remembered that it might possibly be the last one I ever write you. I also remembered that I have known you my entire life and to capture 24 years in three sentences was lazy and spineless. So let's try this again.

I love you in spite of myself and in spite of yourself. I love you beyond any differences that we ever had. Beyond every harsh word, every eye roll, every passive aggressive attack and every nasty thing either of us said. You're my dad. You will always be the guy who drove to my school in a heartbeat every time I got sick and I will always be the girl who followed you around and thought the world of you.

I miss you. There is not a day that goes by that I don't think about you and your stories. The ones that you repeated over and over and I let you because I knew how much you loved to tell them. I miss the guy who sent me to boarding school then came up with an excuse to come and see me every week, the guy who took me to soccer matches and the gym and his lectures and made me help him prepare presentations when I was in primary school and the guy who read through all my varsity essays before I submitted them. The guy who carried a copy of Sunday News in the car because I was interning there and he wanted to show everybody that his daughter was a news reporter.

However, in order to respectfully mourn this guy, I need to be honest with myself. I'm still trying to figure out how to grieve without lying to myself about our relationship. When it was good, it was beautiful. But it wasn't always beautiful. And I could easily point fingers and blame you for all of it. Or I could take part of the responsibility. Come to the acceptance that perhaps I should have chosen understanding over anger. That perhaps I was too quick and too resolute in my anger, that I closed too many doors way too quickly and maybe I took up fights that weren't mine.

I realise now that I only knew you as my dad and not as an individual with wants and needs and dreams of their own. I should have taken time to know you; to learn who you were before you became my dad. What you wanted as a boy, what scared you as a young boy, what hurt you, what made you laugh. Perhaps if I had known these, I would have been a much better daughter to you.

There are things I will never get to say to you but I hope that somehow you know that I wish we both could have done better. That I could have tried better, practiced understanding and patience because I owed you that much. I pray every day that you found peace because in spite of your faults and in spite of mine, you deserve a world of peace. And while you find peace, I will make sure you are never forgotten. I'm starting this thing where I say your name everyday so that you are never really gone. I swear I will make you proud. And I swear I'm okay and I will continue to be. You just get your rest.

I love you daddy.

FRIENDS

"Friendship is the hardest thing in the world to explain. It's not something you learn in school. But if you haven't learned the meaning of friendship, you really haven't learned anything."

– *Muhammad Ali*

To My Best Friend

I always tell you that if you die, I will kill you. I mean it. You know me and killing an already dead body is definitely not the craziest thing I have ever suggested. Don't die. If you did, I don't know what I would do with myself. So still, don't die.

I think about the girl I met 12 years ago and how there is still so much of her in you and yet at the same time that girl is long gone. I am glad I got to meet her and I am glad that I met her when I did. It's funny how if one thing had gone a different way, we wouldn't have met. I'm happy we did though. I think God put you in my life for a reason.

You move people. Half the time you don't realize it because I suppose it comes naturally to you. You are the kind of person that people can't help but want to be around. Your energy is so infectious and so warm and when I'm not basking in that warmth, I am watching from a distance, simply blown by how much fun and beauty you radiate.

Thank you for always being there. Thank you for being honest even when I didn't want honesty, thank you for laughing with me at the weirdest times and crying with me when all I could do was cry. Thank you for just getting me. I never have to explain anything to you because half the time, you're thinking the same thing. Thank you for never judging me, you know literally everything there is to know about me and not once have I ever felt judged.

You're brilliant in all the right ways and I find myself looking forward to seeing how you eventually turn out. I know it will be beautiful but it's just the how that I am so keen to see.

In fifty years, we will be old and rich and drinking expensive tea and you will still be my favorite person to laugh with, to gossip with to swap notes with. And even then when we are old and gray, I will still remind you "Don't die, because I will kill you".

To My Girl Squad

You beauties are the most intelligent, most insightful, most honest group of people. I am so lucky to call you my friends. I wish all of you the very best. I know we don't see each other as much as we would like to. But I trust you are all kicking a respectable amount of ass.

To My Guy Squad

Y'all drive me crazy all the time but I know that I wouldn't trade you guys for anything. Thank you being there for me in different ways. Thank you for letting me make you talk about boys. Thank you for being patient when I was being nosy. Thank you for sharing your spaces and your lives with me.

I always felt protected because I knew you would never let anything happen to me. We don't spend that much time as a group but I'm grateful for the time you shared with me. Grateful for the (albeit terrible) advice and for the many times you showed up for me.

I love you, both as a group and even more as individuals.

To My First Friend

It's been close to 20 years since we first met in that grade one class and decided we would be friends. It's been so long now I don't even remember what brought us together in the first place but I will always appreciate you.

Our little girl memories are some of the fondest and every time I see a pair of little girls playing together, I see a bit of us in them. And I always want to tell them to treasure the time that they have together. I want to tell them that life will separate them pretty soon and although they will try to remain friends, it just won't be the same again.

I say this with us in mind. How we swore back then that we would be friends forever. And we tried for a while but these things happen and now we are no more than Facebook friends who don't even comment on each other's posts. But I get it.

I just want you to know that I am proud of you and everything you have grown into. Although a lot has changed, you are still the same beautiful, kind spirited little girl who befriended me on the first day of school and I will always be grateful that I first learnt from you what it meant to be a friend.

Love always.

To the friend Who Died Too Young

When Facebook reminds me that the 8th of April is your 25th birthday, I remember for the first time in a long time how tragic it is that you never lived to see it. Then I get mad at Facebook...how dare they? Then I get mad at myself because I'm terribly good with birthdays and how dare I forget yours this year.

Then I remember that the 8th of April isn't your birthday anymore. You won't expect gifts, like the time that boy bought you that teddy, you won't roll your eyes at the impersonal "hbd" some lazy ass will plaster on your Facebook wall and you won't stay up till midnight to see who calls first.

The 8th of April isn't your birthday; the 8th of April is just that-the 8th of April. It's just another 24 hours, the sun will rise, the sun will set. The 8th of April is like the 11th of May now or the 17th of December. It's now just numbers on a calendar and none of it means anything.

And maybe I should be grateful that it's one less birthday to remember, one less birthday message to pull out of my back pocket. But on the 8th of April, on the day you are supposed to turn 25, the people who knew you are reminded how the sun still came up the day after your passing like nothing had happened the day before. The people who remember you also remember how the ground complied when they dug it up for you, as if, for it, eating up a 22 year old was all in a day's work.

The grass kept growing, the wind kept blowing, and someone had their baby that day. I think we even made small talk on the way to the funeral, none of it about how unnatural the reason for our gathering was.

Then I think maybe worse things have happened but then I also think worse things haven't happened to people I know. So maybe this too should have stayed there-with all the people I don't know. So maybe this shouldn't have happened to you-it should have happened to somebody else. But that somebody else also would have been somebody else's daughter or somebody else's sister-somebody else's somebody else.

That somebody else probably would have had somebody else writing a letter years later to still try to make some kind of sense out of the whole thing or to make themselves feel less guilty about that blue tick they gave you-because they always "knew" they would pick up the conversation some time later.

So maybe it's okay that it wasn't somebody else. Maybe there are reasons, maybe someday it will make sense. Maybe in the future when we are older, it will make sense. Because all you were-all you are-is a child.

To The Friend I No Longer Speak To

We haven't been speaking for close to two years now and the fact that I have not for a single moment missed you shows me that I dragged our whole friendship for way longer than I should have. I use the term friendship very loosely because as I think about it, ours wasn't a friendship. It wasn't even an alliance. It was two people, who spoke the same language and figured that meant we should spend time together. It didn't mean that. Outside of that, we had no business being around each other.

Earlier, I said something about us not being friends. I remember how it was always me giving and you taking and you never saying so much as a "thank you". I remember me taking up your battles with people because you asked me to. I remember being mad at people because they treated you poorly. I remember losing my friendship with one of your exes because he made you cry. I walked out of that friendship because that's what a supportive friend does. I also however remember you hanging out with a boy I was no longer speaking to because "you loved him".

I never called you out on this because I rationalized it and told myself that my friend would never do something to upset me. So I let it slide, until I learnt you were speaking to yet another boy I wasn't speaking to. This isn't even about boys. We're both better than that. It's about you and your underhanded dealings and your passive aggression and the resentment that I think you always felt towards me although I do not know what brought it on.

I'd be wrong to pretend that it was all toxicity and selfishness and you playing the victim. It wasn't. There were good times. Times when we laughed so hard we fell to the floor. Times when we shared some good gossip, times when we hung out with our friends and talked about a shitload of stuff and times when you were present for me- as present as you could be I guess. I'm not going to pretend four years of friendship were all horrible.

I hold no ill intention towards you. I do however hope you have grown and continue to grow. I have no desire to know you any further after this but I do wish you well and I hope all your dreams come true.

To My Roommate

I know we only find each other together in this room due to a technicality but this is one technicality I will always be grateful for. I know at first or even second glance, I don't look like much, but I swear as far as roommates go, I am pretty badass. I have the recommendations to back it up.

Let's get a few deal breakers out of the way, I snore so your best bet is to make sure you fall asleep before me every single night. On the worst days, I will talk in my sleep. I'm also a bit of a mess, which means every now and then you will find things in places they shouldn't be. I play my music a little loud when I take my showers and my friends are also a little loud.

But for every deal breaker, I swear there's an upside to living with me, I will wake you every morning, and make sure you are never late, I will undo your braids and I will help wash your hair, I will talk about boys with you and I will gossip with you. I will be nice to your friends and give you the room when you need space.

As the person who is the first to see me when I wake and the last to see me before I sleep, you will have an understanding of me that most people won't and this will go both ways. You will see how my face lights up when I talk to my mother on the phone, you will hear me argue with my dad about money and you will appreciate how comfortable my tongue gets when it slides back to the first language it knew. This will go both ways, I will watch you fight boyfriends, I will watch you wash your makeup off everyday. I will know the intimate details of your life. I promise to safeguard them as sacred. To speak on them to you when you need me to and to look the other way when that is what you need.

Sometimes you may hear me crying in the middle of the night, my only request is that you let me be, I will be fine in the morning. And in the morning when I wake up and I am still not okay, I promise that I will fake it for you, because you don't deserve some whiney bitch in a foul mood, you deserve me, a ray of sunshine. At times, I won't be able to hold it in until the lights are off and I may cry in front of you. I apologise in advance for that but I thank you in advance for being there and telling me that it will be okay and I thank you for your discretion- for keeping this to yourself.

You will soon learn that my interactions with a lot of people are unconventional. Again thank you for your discretion. And while we are assigned to each other only for the duration of the semester, I really do hope we become friends even after the technicality has worn out.

To My Best Male Friend

I would have addressed this "To my guy besty" but *uyabazi abantu*.

I always think about how we met and how we had no business staying friends after that but we did anyway and for that I will always be grateful. I will never forget how a guy who was friends with a guy I knew became one of the most important people in my life. And sure, for the most part of our relationship, I am doing most of the talking, and you're pretending to listen but I have come to the realisation that that is the beauty of you. You see people. And you listen.

You have the integrity of no one I have ever met before and I often find myself looking to you to be my moral compass. I am grateful for the many times I have spent ranting about my life and you not once complaining about it. I'm grateful for your insights although sometimes harsh, they are always honest. You have been hands down the most consistent guy in my life and I don't take any of that for granted. You have watched me through some of my lowest turns, my most dysfunctional phases; you have supported my questionable decisions, because our relationship has always been more important than being right.

And life happens and we're growing up and I hate that our best days are behind us. But I know that regardless of how much time we spend apart or how long we go without talking, you will never not have my back. You will never not answer when I call. You will never not waste an opportunity to playfully judge my choices. The same way I will always be here to listen to you, laugh at you, and judge you because it all comes from the purest form of love.

I hope you meet a girl someday. Somebody who understands you and your nuances and appreciates that anything with you takes time, because you deserve it. I wish you nothing but the best and I can't wait for the day when you've made the absolute best of yourself and

I will be there front row centre, clapping like an idiot because I have never for a second doubted how great you would turn out.

To The Friend I Hit Puberty With

So sometimes I go to your Instagram page and I just stare. Don't worry it's not creepy staring. It's just me staring in awe at how different you look from the friend I made ten years ago. Granted you still have the same energy that everybody loves about you, you're still confident beyond belief and you still have the most infectious laugh of anyone I know. However, looking at you now, no one would believe that I spent most of our study periods popping pimples out of your face.

Remember when you got your first beard and we were both so excited, we christened it "Nick" and swore you would never shave it off and now years later, you're an honorary beard gang member and I can't help but think back on the boy who spent hours with me talking about the universe or whatever we knew the universe to be at 15. Thank you for being a sure thing at a time when nearly everything (including my own body) made no sense to me.

You were the first guy to call me beautiful and I don't think it's because you thought I was. Come on, I still have pictures, I was far from beautiful. But you understood the pressure that I was under. You understood the insecurities that I was faced with at that age; wondering if my boobs would ever set in, scared that my period may suddenly appear, and scared that acne would just one day unceremoniously make an appearance. In the middle of that, you managed to call me beautiful. I love you for that.

So cheers to us, for making it through that time, through the boys, the girls, the awkward phases. Thank you for being a constant in the middle of all chaos. I doubt I would have survived puberty if it hadn't been for you and your wit, and our stupid inside jokes and our stupid running gags. I love you. To the glow up and beyond.

To My Newly Married Friends

I love you. I love you in the way that I love Christmas. I am happy when Christmas comes in December. I'll sing the carols, I'll buy the gifts, I'll watch all the Christmas movies. But once January comes around, I am very happy to put away the Christmas lights and get on with my life. And I am happy to not have to deal with Christmas for another eleven months.

I hope this analogy makes sense to you. I'm not saying I only want to see you once a year, I'm saying it's just easier if I do. I am genuinely happy for this chapter of your life that you have entered. A chapter with in-laws and diapers and car pools and things I know absolutely nothing about. I'm happy for your new found happiness but I hate what it does to me. It makes me question a lot of things about myself. It makes me feel like I am falling behind on life, like my shit isn't together. And when I see you with your partners, I can't help but feel pressure to find something similar.

I want to be present for this time of your life but it's just so hard. I can't think of a single thing to say to you. Our priorities are so different right now. And while I love your kids- I genuinely do not think cuter kids exist, I still do not want to hear about them every day. Sometimes I just want to have a conversation with my friend. The friend who used to do some outrageous stuff, who stayed up with me and bitched about boys and nearly started fights with me. I need that back. Even for just one day.

So I hope you understand why you can't be an everyday thing for me. Although I love you to death, I need some kind of distance from you. While this is a huge step in the next chapter of your life, I can't help but feel like I'm being left behind.

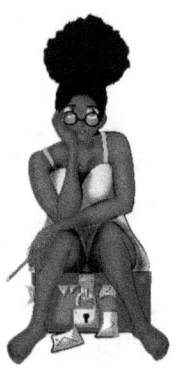

BOYS

"I've never known the lovin' of a man
But it sure felt nice when he was holding my hand
There's a boy here in town says he'll love me forever"
-*The Band Perry*

To The One Who Would Have Been The One That Got Away

I saw you yesterday and we both smiled. Politely, Quietly. Then that was it. Four years of mind games and maybes and almosts and this is what it came down to. I almost didn't smile, you know. I almost walked right past you, almost pretended you didn't exist like I've been doing the past year, but come on, my denial is only so strong. I can't pretend when you're right there-in the flesh.

I'm waiting for that text. The "good seeing you" text or call or something-just anything. Anything to assure me that even if things didn't work out the way we (well at least the way I) wanted them to, I still deserve more than just a smile and wave across the street.

I'm not trying to get you back (not that you ever were mine to get back) but I don't want a smile and wave to be enough for you. I want you to want to have a conversation with me, to tell me how your week was, to share a joke with me, or even share a cup of coffee. Hell, I might even want to meet "her".

Sometimes I feel like we might still be friends but then I remember everything we said and everything we put each other through and...there's just too much to forgive.

And sometimes I feel you're a coward for walking away. I could have made beauty out of you. I could have overlooked everything and let's be honest, there was a lot to overlook. And I never asked you for anything, just to be there, I would have done the rest. I would have done the loving, the caring, the giving, the forgiving, I would have done all of it, all you had to do was be there to be loved and cared for and given and forgiven. I would have done the heavy lifting. Because you meant that much.

I guess none of that matters now but I will always feel like I invested so much of myself into you that I am still hoping I get something out.

That something doesn't have to be you, because I am sure in my heart of hearts, I don't even want you. I just want to have something to show for the time I spent running after you and making a complete idiot of myself for you.

Or maybe I make too much out of this. Maybe I give our interaction a lot more credit than it deserves. Maybe I've put it on a pedestal because memory does that. Maybe it really meant nothing. So I guess I get why I haven't received the "good seeing you" text. I understand why that smile and wave are enough for you.

To The One Who Actually Got Away

You probably won't read this and I totally understand. I just really wish you would. I am sorry. I know I have said this a hundred times and I would say it a hundred times more if I thought it would make a difference. I am sorry. Being 17 and having big words like "love" thrown your way is a pretty scary thing. I am not saying it is an excuse. All I am saying is I was a kid and I didn't know what to do with emotions that big. I know you were also just a kid too but you have always been so emotionally mature and that's why we worked. I am sorry.

I don't blame you for acting towards me the way you do now. I understand perfectly. We had something pretty great- as great as school kids could have anything but it was decent and I ruined it. So I understand why you never want to entertain me beyond common decency and politeness. It just hurts sometimes how guarded you are around me and how aloof you get and how you keep me at a distance and I know why you do it, it just doesn't make it any less hurtful.

I understand it but I just wish you wouldn't do it. I know how entitled that sounds. I don't get to decide how my actions affect you and I sound so selfish expecting to be forgiven by you. It's terrible, I know but I just need a chance. I am not that scared little teenage girl anymore. If you allowed yourself to get to know me as I am now you would realize how much I have grown, how much more I appreciate people and how I still get scared. But I don't run anymore when I get scared.

The truth is if you gave me a chance right now or a whiff of it, I would take it and I would run miles with it. And I would love you so honestly, so fully, so completely with reckless abandon- the way only you deserve to be loved. The truth is you are still the best person I know. The smartest, the hardest working, and the most progressive thinking person who will always have my respect. And if you let me, I would tell you that you are still the most beautiful boy I have ever laid my eyes on.

To The Girl He Loved Before Me

There's a way he looks at me, I'm pretty sure he's convinced it's genuine adoration or something sentimental like that. He means well.

But I know what it is-that look on his face. It's wonder. Wondering if I'm ever going to live up to you and everything you made him feel. Every time I tell a story, he's on the edge of his seat, hoping it'll be as funny as the stories you told him. I watch him die a little inside every time he realises that I'm not that deep, not like you.

You-he never talks about you and I can't bring you up. I'm not that girl. I'm not insecure enough to spend time obsessing over a girl he used to know. I'm not the kind of girl to stay up all night wondering how pretty you are neither am I kind of girl who writes letters like this, and yet here we are.

There's so much I don't know about you, like your name for starters. The one time he spoke about you, he didn't say it. Like it was too precious to be said to the likes of me. I'm competing with a ghost here and I hate it. Give me a name or a face or something, anything to go on. You're a mystery, mystery is beautiful and I can't compete with beauty.

I'm a hell of a girl, but you...You must be something to have caught and kept his attention for that long (yes he mentioned how long that one time he spoke about you).Don't get me wrong, I'm not jealous. I'm enchanted by the mystery that is you. You had everything that I have and you could walk away from it. It takes a certain kind of person to do that.

So bear with me admiring you while I bear with him trying to get over you.

To The One I Failed To Make It Work With-Twice

I've been telling myself and anyone who will listen how mad I am at you and I only realized today that I am not. I really hope you're doing okay and living the life that you always wanted. A life with a wife and a couple of kids and I am glad you got that. I realize now how selfish it is of me to be upset by news of your engagement. You could have very well offered me that same life and we both know I would have run in the opposite direction- kicking, screaming and yelling "fire!"

I will confess however where my anger was coming from. I was mad because I still think it was a little too soon for you to have moved on to a point of wanting to get married. Mad because you are totally winning this break up, there is no way I can top an engagement, try as I might. A part of me was mad that it wasn't me. Another part of me was mad that the door is really closed this time, we can't be saved anymore but the bigger part of me was mad because I had to find out on Facebook.

But whatever I was mad about, I'm not mad about it anymore. Because the truth is I am genuinely happy for you. I remember how much you wanted an organic family and I am so glad you finally got what you wanted. I was going through my things earlier and I ran into a letter you wrote me. And it made me smile. Then I remembered how long it has been since anything about you made me smile and it has been way too long.

I cannot you begrudge you your happiness because even as we began our relationship, we always knew it wasn't forever. It's not like we didn't try, we did, and really hard. But at the end of the day, we were different people who wanted different things and that's okay. This is not me asking for friendship, you and I were never friends. Perhaps that's why this could never work out but that doesn't matter anymore.

I am so proud of you and I wish you all the happiness in the world. Do I still think it was too soon? Yes. But there's no statute of limitations on these things so okay.

To The One I Broke

I am sorry. I think that's all there is to it. I am sorry. Sorry doesn't fix anything but I just feel better knowing that I said it. I know you must think I haven't changed. You just read that apology above and decided that I'm only apologizing to make myself feel better. The truth is, that may be accurate but I'm apologizing for myself as much I am apologizing because I genuinely see the error of my ways.

I have no excuse for the way things played out between us and I could try to rationalize things for you but I would be lying and you deserve better than that. For what it's worth, I never at any point lied to you about anything and believe it or not you're actually one of few people who got the best parts of me.

I understand that this means nothing especially considering that even those allegedly good parts didn't stick around for you. If I could undo anything, I would probably just go back to the day I met you and I would not speak to you. It would save you a lot of pain and me a lot of guilt.

I really hope you don't project any of my nonsense on to whoever has your attention these days. I hope you learn to give people a chance and I hope you accept that I was in fact the problem and that there is nothing wrong with you. I pray you give every little bit of that giant heart to someone who truly deserves it. And I hope you have stopped asking yourself what you did wrong. The answer is nothing. I had issues, and granted I'm still working through them, trying to be better every day. It was nothing you could have fixed.

I promise that this letter is the last piece of communication you will ever receive from me. I won't be texting "hey you" after months of silence, I won't hawkishly comment "she seems nice" when you post her, I won't just check up on you. I am cutting you loose from this cycle that I have forced you into. It always leaves you hopeful and me feeling like crap. You deserve to be let go and that is a kind of peace that I owe you.

I wish you well. And again, I am sorry.

To The One

I don't think a letter will do this situation any justice. I want to send you Michael Buble's "Haven't Met You Yet" but I'll probably play it for you anyway. My journey to you hasn't been easy but I am glad to come to you as I am now not as I was before. I am so glad you are the person who gets this me. I am coming to you as a whole person, leaving behind every broken promise and every disappointment and coming to you with an open heart and an open mind and in sheer faith that this which we are getting into means something.

I just know that this will be different, you won't be another footnote in my story, you will be the climax of it. And page by page, we will write our story. It most certainly won't be perfect but I can promise it will be beautiful. Along the way, things will be said that can't be taken back and a lot will be done which will be hard to forgive but I promise that as long as you are here and as long as you are trying, I am staying here and trying along with you.

I can't wait for all our firsts because that's what we have ahead of us: a world of firsts. First kisses, first fights, first farts, first time we realise we love each other. And I know you are somewhere in the world, maybe writing a similar letter or maybe you're booed up with somebody thinking that's the real deal. Whatever the case, I am here working so hard to finally someday be the person you deserve to come home to.

I'm learning how to deal with emotion and learning to be selfless and learning not to project the past onto other people. I have made slow progress but baby you would be so proud of how far I have come. And when we are finally together, we will both realise how worth it it was for it to have taken so long. Take care of yourself. Take care of your heart and your mind. They are possibly the best parts of you.

And in the words of Michael Bublé, "I promise you kid, I'll give you so much more than I get. I just haven't met you yet".

To The One Who Gets This Version Of Me

I have been reading a lot of books that tell me to stop apologising. They say women apologise too much and maybe I'm betraying an entire gender by doing this but I am sorry.

I am sorry that this is the version of me you have to deal with. The responsible thing on my end would be to cut you loose and let you go because me, in this current state is not a person that should even be attempting to be in a relationship. But life gets lonely and it's nice to know that at the end of the day you will always be there to call me pretty and feign emotions like love and I think I need that.

I guess what I am trying to say is I am a work in progress. The progress is too little and too slow and until that progress starts to pay off, this is my apology in advance. I don't trust people. I figure you have noticed the subtle things like how I roll my eyes when you call me beautiful or how I bring up your past relationships whenever you try to have a serious moment with me. I know for a fact you noticed how I wouldn't speak to you for days after the first time you said you loved me.

I wish I could do better, I wish I could be the person that you need me to be: the girl who calls you because she misses you, the girl who says she loves you and means it. The girl who doesn't pretend to be sick on the day she is supposed to meet your family. I really wish I could give you more. But not right now honey. There is a lot that I am trying to figure out and yours is just a case of terrible timing.

I should just let you go because the truth is you don't stand a chance. You're not up against some guy with a six pack and an accent. It's me you are up against. Me and my defences and my traumas and my prejudices and…it's a lot. You check all the right boxes in so many ways but you can't win this. I'm sorry.

To The Girl He Chose Over Me

You don't know me but I know you. Yes, I cyber stalked you so let's get that awkwardness out of the way very quickly. To be clear, I didn't stalk you because I am creepy; I did so because I am human. Curiosity is the human affliction. And I was curious to know your appeal. See, I don't like losing so I had to figure out what I had lost to.

Then I saw your profile and it made sense. I'll admit it was a little underwhelming but I got it. The sundresses, the inspirational quotes, the family photos! Again, slightly underwhelming but makes a lot of sense. You look like the kind of girl who sings and is good with people and you're definitely the kind of girl that people would believe if you said you prayed.

Know what happens when I tell people I pray? They laugh! I don't take it personally anymore but this isn't about me. This is about you and your singing and your prayers and your wholesomeness. Because at the end of the day, that's what everybody wants right? Wholesomeness! And that's the one thing I could never give. So I get why it's you and not me.

He needs somebody like you. Somebody like you, someone who will ~~enable~~ encourage him, someone who will hold his hand and someone who will bring out the best in him- not what I did. See, he and I are...complex for lack of a better word. When we're good, we're amazing. Then there's part of us that just wants to hurt the other. I think it's because we both know that despite how much we like each other, we know we are no good for each other. "Maybe that's what happens when a tornado meets a volcano."

The fact that I am quoting Eminem just speaks to my point. He doesn't need somebody who quotes Eminem at the drop of a hat. He needs structure and safety and that's what you provide. He, much like me thrives on chaos and you can help him rise above that. Now our boy gets bored pretty quickly, especially when the chaos that he lives off of is no longer there. He may get bored and he may come looking for me again. Now for your sake, more than mine; when this boredom kicks in, I pray that I am evolved enough to not answer. Because I deserve better. You do too and so does he.

To My Most Consistent Booty Call

You sir are doing what you were put on this earth to do.

Never change.

To My Crush

Hie. I was born on the 6th of September. I'm an unapologetic Virgo. My Myer Briggs personality type is INTJ which means I have an introverted Intuitive Thinking and Judging personality- what the Myer Briggs describes as the architect. As of 2016, I have an IQ of 126, I speak 4 languages and I understand about 6 languages. My love language however is words of affirmation.

I'm an indoor girl, I love books and television and movies and music but I also like to get out once in a while. I love old music almost as much as I love Karaoke. I have a new found interest in photography although I am terrible at it. It gives me peace though so I'll keep at it. I also love long walks and long talks about God and the universe and how the world works. I love to laugh and I love animals.

My deal breakers are fake accents, smelly feet and poor treatment of service people. I also do not think we will get along if you are dishonest and not open minded. More deal breakers include but are not limited to: a failure to keep time, bad grammar, use of shorthand, dislike of children, wearing closed shoes without socks on and pushiness.

The pros of dating me are: I am hilarious. I am supportive. I am an incredible listener and I will always help where I can. I am incredibly insightful and if you need me to, I will get along so well with your friends and family. If they mean a lot to you then I swear I will try. I'm also very protective of the people that I love. Once I got you, I got you. I like to write love letters and leave little hand written notes. I also love to give people gifts. The look on someone's face when they open a gift is priceless. I'm also big on acts of service. I'll go on that errand run for you.

The cons of dating me are I am impatient, I am unreasonably guarded and I can be blunt at times. I also totally shut off when I feel like I am not being appreciated the way that I should be. I'm also a little passive aggressive so there will always be that. Lastly, I tend to overthink everything.

So yeah. That's pretty much it. Are we doing this or *kanjani?*

To The Entanglement

For the longest time, I took great pride in how we were always friends first and everything else that did and didn't happen between us was secondary. And then I consider how underwhelmed I am by you lately and I just don't get it. Well, I took my time and thought about it and here's the thing. Granted we were friends and I never wanted you to be more than that. However, I also didn't want this to be enough for you. I wanted you to want me to be more, despite the fact that I didn't want to be.

Anybody else would be a little thrown by this. But you know me. And I know this will not come as a shock to you. You're aware of my self-importance and my narcissistic tendencies and you have called me out on them a couple of times. So while you may not fully understand this, I know it does not come as a shock to you. You see this little cold war that may or may not be going on between us- I know I started it and you just went with it because even I realise that my shenanigans are getting old and you are getting tired of them.

I guess that I resent the fact that you don't want me like that. Because I gave you the best parts of me. I laughed and cried and got mad and got excited in front of you. I showed you myself in all her fullness. The highs, the lows, all of it and you still didn't want me. We're not even friends anymore. You're just some guy who no longer cares about me and I'm the girl who just keeps upsetting you because I'd rather you hate me than feel nothing towards me. So I keep fighting you. Fighting over nothing. Because we have nothing else left. Well I am tired now. This is done. It's not your fault and it's not mine.

It's just that you know so much about me and you got parts of me that most people don't and walking away from this, from you, feels like a betrayal to myself. But I'm letting this go. It's been a wild ride.

Au revoir et bonne chance.

To the Girl We Cheated On

I want to do this right. I want to say the right thing, express the right emotions, and handle the situation as delicately and as tastefully as possible. After all, we are both respectable people. I want to say something like I was young and dumb and maybe I made a mistake because that would earn me some absolution, right. But mistakes typically only happen once. A part of me wants to lie to you and say I didn't know you existed. Then there's the part of me that wants to pull a cliché like "hurt people hurt people". I could say that I grew up around infidelity so that's me projecting...but even that would be a load of bull and you know it.

Truth is it had nothing to do with me being young or being hurt or...truth is I didn't care. I saw something that I wanted and I took it. It had nothing to do with you. It's just a coincidence that what I wanted or who I wanted just happened to be with you at the time. It wasn't a direct attack towards you because truthfully, I don't know enough about you as a person to launch a personal attack against you. And while I am genuinely sorry for the distress that the situation may have caused you, I do not apologise for anything that I may have done to make myself happy. And I use the word happy very loosely here, it wasn't about some profound happiness at the end of the tunnel, it was never going to last. It was about me doing what I wanted and I make no apologies for it.

Ultimately, I don't think I should be the one having this conversation with you. To be fair, you and I are strangers and I owe you absolutely nothing. And I know you and your friends are going to read this together and you're going to agree that I'm a horrible girl and how unsisterly it was of me to "steal" him away from you and how unsisterly it is for me to be this unapologetic about it. You technically cannot steal a person from another person. People make the conscious decision to leave.

But I'm done apologising for things that aren't my fault. I made no commitment to you, so I technically did you no wrong. He should be the person you talk to about this, he should be the person you send hate mail and slut shame and that should be the villain in your story. Not me. I wanted happiness no matter how momentary and I took it where I thought it was to be found. It is unfortunate that it came at the expense of your comfort but again, I am not the bad guy here.

To The Wild Card

We didn't make a lot of sense to a lot of people. We wouldn't have made sense to me either if I wasn't in the situation. Oh but the sense we made! I remember the first time I saw you. Tatoos, drunk out of your mind and yet so effortlessly confident. That was the moment I decided, I had to have you.

Again, nobody understood it. Why would the overachieving smartass in glasses want to hang out with you but I knew why I wanted to be around you. You represented everything I wanted to be. I would have given almost anything to be like you. To not have a single care in the world, to be so sure of myself that it did not matter what anyone thought of me. I could not be you, even on my best days and for over a year, I lived vicariously through you.

Thank you for sharing your space with me. Thank you for letting me follow you around and thank you for pretending that I was as interesting as you are. We both know I wasn't. And I also know that I wasn't the kindest when the novelty wore off. Perhaps instead of being enamoured with the rebellious side of you, I should have realised that this side came with its own set of problems.

A person who is drunk the first two times you meet them is very likely to be drunk the next time you see them and the time after that. A person who doesn't care what people think of them still won't care even when you are in public with them. I shouldn't have tried to change you. Lord knows I couldn't.

I'm sorry for the many times I got mad at you for being yourself. I apologise. Were there obvious problems with who you were? Yes. But those weren't mine to fix especially if they were the things that attracted me to you. I had no right to be frustrated with you over things that were so typically you.

I miss you sometimes but I know how that ends. I will be angry all over again and you will be tired of my anger all over again. I just hope you're doing okay.

To Guys Leaving Me On Read

Yaz liyadelela.

But I will get so pretty one day and you will wish you had responded to my texts.

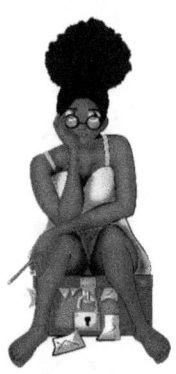

GOD

"In articulo mortis (At the moment of death)
Caelitus mihi vires (My strength is from heaven)
Nearer, my God, to thee,"
-*BYU Vocal Point*

To God

I just want to say that I have never doubted your existence, not for a single second in my life. I think the existence of the universe is a testimony to your being. My entire life is proof that you exist. I know as far as children go, I am far from ideal. But if I have been around for this long, I figure there is something in me that you see that can still be saved, but then again, I don't think you are a God who believes in merit so maybe there really isn't anything redeemable in me. Whatever the case, I am grateful to be alive, grateful to have the opportunity to speak to you. I find I don't speak to you as much as I should. There are so many things that I do want to talk to you about but I never find the appropriate way to say them. Most of these things that I want to say are questions and one lesson that I have been taught, albeit imperfectly is not to question your methods.

I wish my faith had better manners. That it knew to trust you without questioning anything that you do. I do believe in you- you know that, I cannot imagine placing my faith anywhere else but I sometimes wish I knew what your plan was for me, for a lot of things. I guess it's because I am kept out of the loop about a lot of things that affect me. So I guess part of this letter is a request. A request of faith that even when nothing makes sense to me, may I trust that everything that happens to me is all part of a plan.

The thing is lately I have had this thing where I don't know really know where you and I stand. I mean we have always had our troubles. By troubles I mean I have always overreacted to some of the things you do. And you have always given me room to reach because we've always both known that I would come back. I have been trying to find my way back to you for just over a year now and it scares me because for the first time I don't see a way back. Too much has happened and I am trying to move past it but I can't seem to find reconciliation and that breaks me.

I've been drifting for too long and I am scared that if I keep going like this, I may be lost forever. I miss being able to talk to you, I miss knowing you're listening, I miss not being afraid because I knew something much bigger than me was at play. I cannot continue to go through life not believing. And I have tried to find you lately but between the hurt and the anger, I just can't seem to see clearly. So I will wait here because I currently do not have the strength to search. I am begging you now to find me. Find me because I can't find my way to you anymore.

To God, A Thank You Note.

I read our last conversation and in it I was so desperate to be taken back by you that I forgot something very important. I forgot to thank you for a lot of things. I suppose even in my prayers, I sort of rush through this part to get to the part where I ask you for stuff. I'm terrible I know. So this is a thank you note from me to you. Let's start simple:

Thank you for my family and friends. I cannot imagine going through life with any other group of people. You provided me with people who know me, understand me, love me and are honest with me. You gave me parents who provided siblings who were attentive, grandparents who were doting, friends who were supportive, neighbours who were helpful, teachers who were insightful and role models who were always exemplary.

I thank you for the opportunities that you have brought my way. I appreciate every single one of them. Both big and small. It is these little victories, these little moments one by one and one after the other that have contributed into making me the person that I am. It is these opportunities and these little moments of victory that I will look back at when I am old and grey and I will know that you were always preparing my greatest hits.

I thank you for the hard times. Sometimes I get mad at you when these happen but I know that it's all for a higher purpose and there is no coincidence with you. I, like you am a writer and I realise that nobody grows in their comfort zone. So when these things that break my heart and keep me in bed for days happen, I am grateful that I never have to feel pain like that again, grateful that I am a stronger and more insightful person for having experienced it. Grateful even more that I will be a better person for it.

Thank you for my mind. This complex, borderline crazy little companion that you gave me. This mind has done so much for me. It has created whole universes and taken them down. It has held its own in arguments and it is part of the reason I have come as far as I have. It has also saved me from a lot of situations that could have gone south. I am also very grateful for the heart that you gave me. It's big but it's a little shy and that's okay. I thank you that you gave me a heart that was so capable of so much love and also so capable of protecting itself.

Thank you for always being here for me. Thank you for taking me back when I have gone astray. Thank you for listening to my whining. Thank you for never giving up on me. Thank you for seeing me. Thank you for saving me. Thank you for being you.

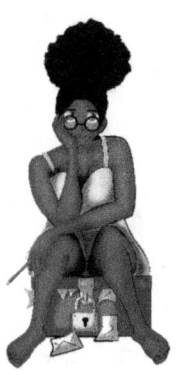

PEOPLE
"Let us recognize that we are all part of each other. We are all human. We are all one."
— *Suzy Kassem*

To You Dear Reader

First off, thank you for buying this book. You just made a girl's dream come true. What you hold in your hand are some of my most honest, most intimate thoughts. I thought about how I could cram the experiences of my life and the people that I met into one document and I decided this would be it.

So I started to think of all the things I never got to say to the many people I met and I thought to write a letter to each of them. Some of these letters were so easy to write because I knew how I felt and the words just came right out.

Some of the letters killed me to write, they made me confront feelings that I have been avoiding and some letters were confusing because what I thought I felt about them didn't turn out to be the way I actually felt.

I hope that in reading these, you realise that your experiences are not so different from my own. I hope in these letters, you find sentiments that seem familiar. But above all, I hope you enjoy reading these letters.

To My Mentor

I don't think I say thank you enough. And I don't think you realize that I don't say thank you enough because you don't realize what you did for me. So this is me thanking you and letting you know how meeting you changed my life. You took a chance on a college kid and I don't take any of that for granted. You could have at any point gone with somebody with more experience, somebody who is better connected, somebody who was more of a sure thing but you went with the wild card and for that I will always be grateful.

I look up to you in so many ways. I look up to your work ethic and how willing you always are to dive headfirst into a new project. I appreciate how no voice is too small for you, how you take ideas and suggestions from literally anyone and try to make them into the best version of themselves. Your door is always open to anyone who is willing to walk through it. I am very often in awe of how much you do for other people. How you are always willing to help even when there is nothing in it for you, how you always hold the door open for the next person to come through.

From you, I have learnt patience, positivity through the worst of times and to always to get the most value out of situations. You have earned my respect and loyalty in ways that very few have. If at any point you need me to work on anything, this is the pledge I am making to you. I don't care how busy I am, if you need me to do anything, I will drop whatever else I am doing or go on four hours of sleep- Lord knows I have gone on less.

Very few people would have taken the chance on me that you did and maybe I did not deserve the chance and maybe I did. All I know is for as long as I can, I will spend my time paying you back for taking a chance on me. And I could turn around and say that I got to where I got because of my talents and hard work but the truth is I wouldn't be here if it wasn't for the kindness that you showed me.

To My Favourite Teacher

I was seventeen and all I wanted was to be you. I remember working so hard on your classes not necessarily because I wanted to pass but because I wanted to make you proud. I remember the first day I saw you and I decided you were who I was going to be. Sure, a lot has changed now but I will always be grateful that you gave a teenage girl someone to respect and look up to.

Thank you for believing in me in times that even I did not have that much faith in myself. Thank you for seeing potential when all I saw was the present moment. They say we all have that one teacher who changes our lives forever and I will always believe that you were that for me.

I remember the first time I said out loud that I wanted to direct movies. I had never said that to anybody before mostly because I was scared of how anyone would react to hearing that. Would you be disappointed? Would you call it silly? Would you think I would fail gloriously at it? Your reaction was so reassuring. You weren't thrown by it in anyway; you just encouraged me to read more on what I would need to pursue it. Many times I think about how differently my life would have turned out if your reaction had not been what it was.

Thank you for being the teacher every student deserves to have. The kind that encourages you, pushes you and when you start to grow a big head, calls you to order.

Eternally grateful.

To The Rest of The world

My name is Nkosilesisa and I would much sooner swallow a razor blade than have you call me Nkosinesisa. I mean it's a cool name, it's just not mine. I do not like being called by names that aren't mine. I do not like being called fat, or nerdy. I particularly do not like being called "Mundevere" but maybe that's just me. I have two left feet, I do not know how to ride a bike, or swim, or play an instrument. I do however know how to drive a whole person insane. Ask my exes, they know what's up.

I love me a pretty boy, pretty with a bad attitude and an even worse IQ. Don't judge, those are the easiest to deal with. I'm told I was fussy as a kid, said too much, too loud- not much has changed. The look on my face will always tell you way more than my words ever will. I have a lot of conversations with myself in my head. And sometimes I have them out loud but I've learnt to end them before people start staring.

I hate it when people stare. It always makes me think something's gone wrong. And my brain always goes to the worst case scenario. Sometimes I think it's my way of making up for the fact that my life will never be as interesting as worst case scenario. Sometimes I think it's one of my many ways of self-destructing because best believe if this girl is going down, this girl is going down on her own terms. I was raised tough but sometimes I send an honest text then send a "lol" immediately after, so maybe I'm not as tough as I like to think. I have abandonment issues. Once I fell off a moving car and as soon as my body hit the ground, my first instinct was to get up and run after the car, in case it didn't stop for me. I ran, bleeding into the same vehicle that had just spat me out.

I like it when I cry. It's like an odd cleansing ritual that I've gotten used to. I like it even more when I make myself cry, because like I said, if this girl is going to hell, she is dragging herself to hell. I believe in hell as I believe in heaven. I believe there is a God in heaven as I believe there's a piece of the devil in each of us. I believe in magic, I believe in miracles and once I paid a dollar and had to believe in psychics and I believe Ed Sheeran when he says we can all be loved the way that God made us. So...hie, I'm just a girl, sitting behind an Acer (because I can't afford a MacBook) and hoping you all are ok with me.

To The Men Staring As I Walk By

I've considered moving to Zambia. I stayed there for a little while and I'm actually entertaining the idea. I could go on about opportunities and cultural exchange and... none of that is my motivation. My motivation is I was told that in Zambia, it is considered sexual harassment to stare at a woman for more than five seconds. You could go to jail for that. And that's it. That's what seals my immigration deal.

See, there's just too many of you staring as I walk by. And I know I'm not a remarkably beautiful girl so there's really not much to stare at. Even if I was, it still wouldn't warrant the staring and the leering. It is uncomfortable, it is invasive, it is rude...you know some of these things just come down to basic manners; it is rude to stare and also don't talk to strangers.

Don't talk to strangers= don't catcall. I have not met a woman who was not disgusted by catcallers. Before you even think of it, no! No woman thinks catcalling is a compliment. So tuck that away now. Strangers yelling beauty at you is not a good thing. I've heard a few guys saying "then how else will you know you look good?" Trust me there is a not a girl on the planet who doesn't know when she looks good. So if you think catcalling will make a girl feel more confident, you are wrong. It actually has the opposite effect.

Y'all ever had a camera held up to your face. Like not the subtle, couple of metres away camera. I mean has anybody held it right to your face and it's staring you square in the face? No? Try it. That's how being stared at by strange men feels. You're too close and too obvious in your staring. And I never know why you are staring or how staring at me makes you feel. I just know that it makes me feel uncomfortable and exposed and I also know there's really nothing I can do about it. God forbid, I tell you where to get off.

I also know it's not entirely your fault. I mean it is your fault that you stare but it's not your fault that you think it's okay to. You are the result of a system that has objectified women for the longest of years. That's what it comes down to, right. You don't acknowledge the fact that the woman walking in front of you is an entire human being with ears and eyes and feelings and reactions. Y'all don't see that, do you?

Honestly speaking, this is not a thing I or anyone I know can change. I do however, hope you read this letter. And I hope that when you have, you really think about your actions. And I hope you eventually learn to do better.

To Girls Worried About Fat and Folds

I'm not going to start telling you you're beautiful. Telling you would suggest that I think you don't know that. But you do. I also don't want to tell you that all body shapes are beautiful. Because 1) you also know that and 2) that's just something skinny people tell us so that we don't revolt.

Anyway, beautiful as you are, it's okay to be worried about certain parts of your body. I know that mini heart attack that you get when you realise you now have four bellies instead of the usual two or you now have three chins instead of the usual one and a half. In an ideal world, these things would not worry you. But *kusemhlabeni*, appearance matters, people see your body before they see your heart or your soul and it's okay if you want your body to look a way that it currently doesn't.

There's nothing wrong with wanting to shed a few kilos, nothing wrong with wanting one chin; after all that is the standard. There is also nothing wrong with the process that you will take to get there. Diet if you want to, exercise, try supplements...do what you need to and want to to get to where you want to be.

In all of this, I hope you do it for the right reasons. I hope you do it above all because you want to. And I hope you want to for yourself. In worrying about this fat and these folds, I hope you are worried that you don't like seeing them on you or they make you feel some type of way. I fully hope this has nothing with someone making a comment about your weight and I hope this has nothing to do with the fact that you didn't grow up seeing a lot of people who look like you being called beautiful.

If this fat and these folds worry you entirely for you, then honey, do what you will. With or without the folds and in spite of the fact that you know it... you are so incredibly beautiful.

To The Guy Who Sexually Assaulted My Friend

Let the record state that in my entire life, I have only been in two physical altercations. The first time was in a combi when this (male) stranger called my friend out of her name. The second was when another (male) stranger pulled a different friend by her hair. You might say that I am good at taking up things that have absolutely nothing to do with me. So this letter should not come as a surprise. You may have also then realised that I am not afraid to throw hands, especially if I'm throwing hands at men with obvious boundary issues.

But if I found you and threw hands at you, then she would never forgive me. So we'll talk. I think you are a coward, a disgusting one at that. I think you are the reason she says she has no interest in boys or men or the institution of sex. You're the reason she coils up anytime she is out after dark, because she is scared she might run into somebody else like you. She doesn't trust anybody anymore and I'm sure you know that has everything to do with you. I have watched her push people away, people who had the very best of intentions for her but no one is ever the same after what you did. So congratulations.

She told me you tried to reach out to her recently...what did you want to say? What could you possibly have to say to her? We can both agree you have done enough. I hope you stop pestering her, let her move on with her life, let her do with your damage what she will; you don't get to be a part of it. Not anymore. I'm not telling you this so that you feel good about your spoils or whatever it is that you do, I'm telling you this so that you know that in spite of you, she will be okay.

She will learn to love and she will learn to live and because of the person that she is, she might even forgive you one day. I will not. I am not that person and take this as warning, should I ever meet you or run into you, I will shout in your face the revolting human being you are and then I will fight you-physically fight you because like I said, I have a problem with men who don't understand boundaries.

To The Varsity Staff Member We Didn't Report

This isn't me "Me Too-ing" you. I have paid enough attention to realise that we don't live in a country where people care about sexual harassment. So relax, you can keep your job. I won't name drop. That's not what I'm doing here. I am just telling you that I have not forgotten what you did. You probably have. I would assume you do it a lot so it's hard to keep track.

I was in my second year when you basically motor boated me. Remember how you said you wanted milk then dipped your oversized, underutilised head in between my breasts before I could even tell you why I was there? No. You probably don't but I do. Up until that moment, I had never been that terrified of an authority figure.

I remember walking out of your office and asking myself if that had really happened. Then I told myself it hadn't because come on, who just sticks their head in somebody's boobs like that? Had to be fake, right? So I let it go. Two years later, you offered to give me and my friend a ride into town. Decent enough, right. Remember how you took a detour to your house for...I don't remember what it was then you made us cook for you? Remember that part?

Remember how you snuck into your kitchen and groped me while I cooked for you then did the same with my friend and then you took us back to school? No town trip for these girls. We didn't talk about it either. What could we possibly say? We most certainly could not talk about it with anybody else.

This isn't you being "Me Too-d". This is your free pass because if I went the "Me Too" route, there would be questions, what was I doing in your office? I was literally there to submit something to your colleague. What were we doing in your car? You offered us a lift and that was good money saved. What were we doing in your house? You took us there.

So you see why this isn't a "Me Too"? There would be way too many questions from people who don't care at all. I mean one of your colleagues didn't even bother to learn our names. He used numbers for his female students. Numbers of how much he thought we weighed. I'm not naive enough to believe that a system that enables a teacher to call a student "70kgs" will help me. So, relax, no "Me Too", no name dropping, your job is safe.

To User ZimboHotboi33 On Instagram

This is the fourth time this week I find a message from you in my DMs. My silence means I do not want to speak to you. Thank you for expressing your desire to get to know me. At this point, or any point in the future, I have no desire to reciprocate. May this be our last exchange?

P.S: Please stop sending me pictures of your junk. It does literally nothing for me - or your case.

To Anyone Working Through Grief

A while ago I posted something on my WhatsApp status. It read "My lowest moment was when I was throwing up, kneeling over a toilet in a club in foreign country and begging Mphatso to listen to me talk about my dead father." I don't like to share personal details all that much because 1) they are personal lol 2) I always think everybody else has their own shit going on- they don't need me piling my stuff on top of theirs. However I felt the need to share this in particular because I thought someone might need to hear it.

Does someone need to know what a lightweight I am? Not what I mean. I continued the post as "Low moments are low but they don't last for long. I think mine was just a couple of minutes, maybe 3, maybe 5." Do you know the line from "The fault in our stars" that says pain demands to be felt? So feel it. While it demands to be felt, the worst kind of pain does not last very long- it doesn't last forever.

Think back on the worst kind of pain you felt. Perhaps when you heard of the loss of a loved one. The very first time you heard it, it hurt, it stung, it nearly killed you but how long did that last? I don't mean the residual pain that stays with you years after. I mean the initial pain...think about it, it really did not last as long as we let ourselves think.

I ended the post by saying "Low moments don't last forever. Once you have gone through it, that's it. It never has to happen again." See, pain and grief are not recurring things. Yes, we lose a lot along the journey of life but no two losses are the same. Ever! That is the silver lining I am going for here, whatever loss you have suffered, you never have to endure again. You will never have to feel a pain like that again. You only get to lose a person once because there is only one of that person. And once they are gone, that's it. Nothing else can hurt you in the way that losing them did.

This isn't a formula for grief-I am possibly the unhealthiest griever on the planet. This is just me saying it gets better. I swear. I'm not going to put a timeline on it because it doesn't work like that. All I am saying is, it will get better.

To Girls Who Lost Their Daddies

It's fathers' day and you don't want to turn such a celebratory event into a pity party for yourself so you post a meme to your WhatsApp status because you are a good sport.

It would have been his birthday today but there are no cards to write and no presents to wrap so you call that boy who knows literally nothing about you and you get drunk with him. He is lazy and uninspired and you know your dad would have hated him but that's kind of the point, it's your own little rebellion. One that nobody else will understand. So you spend 6 August with this idiot because 6 August doesn't matter anymore, it's just as good a day as any to get wasted.

Your friends start looking at you funny after the funeral. They get that you are in pain but they also miss their friend-the jokester. So you start with the orphan jokes, they sting a little but at least nobody is looking at you funny anymore. Besides, you only just stopped being a father's daughter; the rest of your life is still as it has always been.

You cry after every encounter you have with your uncle because although he is wonderful, he looks too much like his brother and has too many of his mannerisms and it's just hard to look at him and not think about your dad.

And while you cry and think about your dad, you start to wonder if you will ever know what it's like to be loved that fully and that completely by a man. Wondering if anybody will ever want the best for you the way that he did? And it will suck knowing that you have probably lived past the fullest form of being loved and wondering if it will ever get any better than that for you.

I don't have the answers. But I can tell you that you will live through it. There will be times when you don't even want to get out of bed, but get out and live. He may be gone but honey you are still here.

To Anyone Who Lost Somebody To Suicide

The first thing you will feel is shock because you don't really believe they would do it. You probably knew that things were bad but you just didn't know how bad they were. The second thing you are going to feel is betrayal, how dare they go through this and not tell you? How dare they choose such a seemingly easy way out? The third thing you are going to feel is anger. You are going to call them selfish and at your lowest, you will feel, well they got what they wanted after all. Then you are going to feel guilty and the guilty phase will last for such a long time and you are going to wish you had been kinder and had been more present and you are going to wish you had been more forgiving or more understanding or... only none that of that will help anybody now.

Death is always tricky, it's so final and scary and cold and lonely and when you think that somebody you knew and loved chose this, it's going to be even trickier. You're going to feel shame at some point. Ashamed that when given the choice between being your parent/child/friend/spouse and being dead, somebody actually chose to be dead. Imagine that- somebody would rather be dead than have to deal with you another day. It will mess up with your view of yourself, were you not enough to stay alive for? Are you the reason they chose to end it all? Did they even think about you when they decided they were done? Why would they do that to you?

I guess the temptation to make the suicide of a loved one be about ourselves is great. The truth, however is it probably wasn't even about you. It hardly ever is. There was probably nothing you could have done to stop it. It had more to do with things that they were dealing with on an individual level. Back to the "was I not important enough to stay for" question, the answer simply is no you weren't. Nobody is that important, nobody is important enough to be the deciding factor in whether or not another person lives or dies. My point is at some point you are going to have to stop making their decision about you.

Along the way, people are going to talk to you about forgiving your loved one. They'll tell you how if you forgive, you will start to heal. Again, this isn't about you, this is not yours to forgive. They didn't take their life *at* you. They did it because they were tired, and hurt and they had had enough of life because let's face it, life sucks at times. It was never about you. It was a person looking for a way out and all you have to do as the person who loved said person is to respect that decision. It does not have to make sense to you and it will make you cry every time you think about it. But this is what I always say; take comfort in that after years of sacrificing and providing and giving, the last thing that they did on earth, they did entirely for themselves. That counts for something.

To Anyone Dealing With Depression

Breathe!

To Body Shamers

I swear that transition from "you're pretty" to "you're pretty for a chubby girl" has humbled me in ways not even menopause will be able to. But I'm used to being humbled especially when it comes to my weight. See when I was a kid, a number of "*sdudlas*" were thrown my way and I really didn't care. So I was little chubby, so what? But as I grew up, I realised sdudla wasn't endearing anymore. Sdudla was an insult. Sdudla was relatives telling me they thought I was older than my sister, Sdudla was one of my aunts saying I would grow old really quickly because of my weight, Sdudla was my classmate saying she thought I would die pretty early if I didn't watch the weight.

Sdudla is people like you, everyday thinking because they look a certain way, they have a right to tell people how they should look. First off, it's terrible manners. Who tf raised you? Second, someone else's body is not an opinion for you to have. I want to go on a tangent about how everybody is beautiful but you all know that. What I have noticed about people like you is that you enjoy telling people like me that we are beautiful but feel a certain way when people like me actually believe we are beautiful.

You tell us we are beautiful and then turn around and frown upon a size 22 in a crop top. "Big girls are beautiful" until somebody in a different size wants to pose in a bikini then suddenly it's about covering it up and the worst of you want to bring Jesus into it. With everything going on in the world, do you really think Christ cares that I wore a stupid mini skirt? Y'all are exhausting. How are you so comfortable telling big girls that they are beautiful but so shaken by them believing that they are?

You'll also tell someone like me "you're not fat, you're beautiful". Why do I have to be one or the other? Why can't I be a beautiful girl who just happens to be fat? Not a beautiful fat girl, (because beautiful fat girls are not a novelty). Not a girl who is beautiful in spite of her fat, just a beautiful girl. Don't explain it, don't make apologies for it, just call me beautiful and let it end there.

Second thoughts, why are you even calling me anything? No man. Mind your own body.

To My Younger Self

You're about to enter a relatively complex part of your life and it won't always be easy. I'm hoping if I leave you this letter it might maybe ease it up a little. Just try to remember everything momma taught you. If you want something, say please, if you're get something, say thank you, if you're hurt, forgive, if you hurt, apologize, if that boy next door tries to touch you, say no, ~~unless you want him to.~~

You and mum aren't always going to get along, but that's ok, it's just a phase, give it a year tops and you'll be as close as ever. Not everything will go your way. People will come in and out of your life, but I'm sure you'll be able to handle it. Remarks will be made, not all of them nice, but they'll make you a stronger person. Promises will be made. Vows will be broken. Not all your friends are going to be forever, and not all your choices are going to be smart. You'll have serious lapses in judgment, they won't cost you much, but they'll sting a little. You'll have to say goodbye to a lot of people who mean a lot to you, and there are certain things that you'll just have to give up.

Sometimes you'll look in the mirror and not recognize yourself and sometimes you'll sit by yourself and realize how far you've fallen. There'll be times when you'll feel alone... you probably will be. You're the best friend you could ever have. There'll be nights when you want to cry yourself to sleep, go ahead, let your tears fall right out of those pretty eyes. Your heart may or may not break a couple of times, but that's also alright...you'll also break a heart or two yourself. And sometimes you'll do things you don't mean to, you'll hurt people when you really don't want to, you'll say things you'll never be able to take back, you're not a bad person, you're just human, beautifully and perfectly human.

But just like Pink says in one of your favorite songs, "Everything will work out just fine."- YOU will work out just fine. This is just a letter that I hope prepares you for what's ahead...who you become is entirely up to you. You're a smart girl-you'll figure it out

To My Future Self

We did it, honey.

To Anyone Who Cares (In Case I Die)

I am sorry I have died. Even more so that I have died at this particular time. I had plans and dreams and shit to do and I suppose some of it involved you. I am sorry I have not stuck around as long as I should have. I honestly would have loved to but there is a plan and a reason and a God in heaven who knows what He is doing.

I am not sure if I have the ability to miss earth form where I am. But if I do, I swear I miss the sound of my mother's loud voice on the phone waking me up every morning. I miss the smell of dog as my puppy licks my face. I miss the sun peeking through my window. Above all I miss the beauty of being alive and being part of life- even as a tiny inconsequential part of it. I miss life.

That's not to say you should feel bad for me. Please don't. Because I lived. I lived the best way I knew how and I have no regrets as far as that is concerned. I loved. Deeply. Stupidly. All too much and yet somehow never enough. I lived out a forgivable portion of my dreams, I made mistakes, some big, most of them really small. Should I ever have regrets, it will be that I spent too much time obsessing over the little mistakes I made. I laughed. Boy, did I laugh. Till my face hurt, till I cried, till I could literally feel my stomach at the tip of my tongue and sometimes till I peed myself a little. So don't worry about me. I lived a full life- as full as I could - given the time that I was given.

Onto worldlier issues: give all my photographs to my mother. Give all my clothes to my sister, if she can't fit in them, have her give them away. If I have any contraband, give it to my brother. Give my humble book collection to my best friend. There are about ten notebooks on my desk. They are filled with ideas and concepts... give them to my boss, he will know what to do with them. Give my sneakers to the boy I love. (Most of them are unisex and I'm pretty sure he can fit in a size 8). I have a memory box in my closet and I don't know what you'll do with that one. Dealer's choice.

In all this, I only ask that you remember me. It sounds like a ridiculous request but life has a habit of going on even under the worst of circumstances. One day you will try to remember the sound of my laughter and you won't. On another day, you'll try to remember which side of my face my half dimple was on and you won't remember. I forgive you. You can forget that. But please don't forget me.

And please don't let the world forget me either. Just find a way of bringing my name up any chance you get. Just don't make it weird. I mean you can only bring up a dead girl so many times before it becomes creepy. Walk that fine line.

Thank you for having taken time to know me. I appreciate you. Till we meet again.

To Girls Who Have Been Called Intimidating

Pretty early on, you will realise that people - male people in particular only have two reactions to you. They either totally hate you or totally adore you. I wish I could explain to you how it happens, but I can't. It happens and that's it. Half of them will find your sarcasm hilarious; they will think your truths are something to learn from or at least something to think about. The rest are just going to think you are a loudmouth or a know-it-all or just a plain ole bitch.

Somewhere along the way you will feel the need to prove to people that you're in fact not a bitch. You'll want to prove that you too are kind and generous and agreeable. Which is okay but the thing is you were never not any of these things. You were always kind and accommodating but because you also had opinions, it was always easier to focus on the parts of you that they couldn't stand.

So you will continue for some time on this journey of being an agreeable woman. Because you're only human and it's nice to be liked. For a while you will do it all. You will bite your tongue when somebody says something you know to be wrong - where ignorance is bliss, right. You will smile politely at their sexism, you'll nod when they start to spew yet another grossly misguided opinion, you will respond graciously even when their interactions are predatory. Then one day you will get tired of it and then it'll start all over again and you'll be back to being the bitch.

They will go back to talking shit about you to their friends yet spend the night texting you. They will never acknowledge your presence to their friends but when it's just the two of you they'll want to know every intricate detail of your life. And you will let this slide, you will rationalise it. Ultimately, you know that girls like you are not the kind of girls that someone would ordinarily claim. You are not agreeable enough, your faces are too loud and your opinions stare people too hard in the face.

He will say his friends think you're a ball buster and that's why he can't be seen with you. You are a sweet enough girl to talk to but too hard to bring around the boys. So you let yourself become their dirty little secret. Joke's on them though, you're talking to the entire friend group and you know not a single one of them will get anything out of you. I've been where you are. I've let people call me beautiful one minute and then turn around and pretend I am invisible because I didn't fit the mould of what they wanted me to be. I have had people let their friends disrespect me then turn around and call me "baby" when nobody was listening.

You deserve better. Better than to be someone's archived message and dirty secret. You deserve more than "No one can find out" and "Leave now, I'll follow you in twenty minutes". You're so much more than that. You're the kind of girl people write books about. The kind of girl I would never insult by calling a queen-queen just means you were born into the right family or married into the right family. You are the kind of girl who earned every piece of land you walk on. You're a gladiator, a contender, a trailblazer and anyone who is intimidated by that should take several seats.

To Black Girls

I recently read a poem by Omar Holmorn. It is called "Ten Things I want to say to a black nerd." So I decided to write this to you, brown skinned girl. Ten things I want to say to a black girl:

1. You are beautiful. Incredibly beautiful.
2. Even then, your beauty should never be the most interesting thing about you.
3. Laugh, life isn't that bad.
4. Love, sure it may hurt sometimes but you will never regret having loved.
5. Smile, it really costs nothing.
6. Believe, I don't care what it is but find something to have absolute faith in.
7. Fight; stand up for what you believe in. Stand up for yourself. Stand up for the little guy.
8. Actually fight. Throw a punch once in a while. People are exhausting.
9. Spend time with your mother.
10. The world does not like or protect you as much as it should. So you better like yourself and protect yourself enough for the whole world. More so, you better like your black sisters and protect them because the world doesn't like or protect them all that much either.

To The Struggling Artist

I'm in no position to tell you what to do, I still think of myself as a struggling artist and I don't know if reading this letter will help you in any way. But I'm just going to put it out there. You will do with it what you will.

Let's get the nastiness out of the way quickly. Your first pieces of work will suck. That is a given. Try as you might, they will be terrible. The upside is they won't feel that way when you first do them, you will be proud of them and they will be your babies. What they will teach you is discipline and they will give you an idea of what the rest of your life is going to be like. It is at this stage that you decide whether to stick around or jump ship. Both are respectable decisions.

Your early years will also test your discernment and you'll find yourself at a lot of crossroads...should I take something up even if I don't believe in it but it pays well? Should I do something I really enjoy even if it won't pay? My advice would be go with the latter. What makes art beautiful is how much of yourself you put into it. If you enjoy it, the joy you get out of it will be more fulfilling than any amount of money. But then again, you will need to eat so...decisions decisions.

Granted this art thing takes hard work and commitment and perseverance...cool. But I think there's a lot more that goes into being an "artist". I think you need a highly inflated ego to think you can pull off being an artist. Because not only are you asking people for their attention, you're asking them to pay you for their attention.

You also need a certain level of delusion when it comes to you and your talents. Because let's face it, artists are basically paid to do what everybody else can do. So you need to believe that you do these things so exceptionally well that you should be paid for it. What I mean is every human is born with the ability to sing (musicians), with the ability to lie (actors) with the ability to narrate a story (writers) and with the gift of memory (photographers).You need to be deluded enough to believe that your inherent gift, which everybody else has is deserving of special attention than everybody else's.

Lastly you need a certain level of narcissism. Every person has a view of the world. But you need to believe that yours is the view deserving of attention for the length of a 90 minute film or a 90 page book or a 90 second song. My point is...humility is good, but as an artist humility can't be your strongest trait. Because your entire livelihood is based on the assumption that your understanding of the world is more intimate than most people's. You have to believe that you are better or chosen or special to pull this art thing off.

And I know that words like ego and narcissism and delusion are usually terrible words but in this case, they are things that you may need to survive. Most times you will have to rely on yourself more than anybody else. You'll have to be your biggest cheerleader, you'll need to be your biggest hype man and that's when narcissism and delusion and ego will have to come in.

To The Public Income Kid In A Private School

There's a scene in the first episode of Scandal's Season 3 where Rowan tells Olivia that she has to work twice as hard to get half of what everybody else has. If there is any way I can get you to remember this at all costs, then please let me know and I will send you a text every day with these exact lines, I will get you the mp3 version of the scene so that you play it over and over again, if that means you will never forget. Twice as hard for half of what they have.

You've been thrown in the deep end and you possibly know even without saying anything to anyone that you're an outsider. So you know its sink or swim. Swim. I hope you can. I don't mean metaphorically swimming. I mean literal swimming. Sport is big in this universe you have entered and it helps that one be able to swim. In any case, if you can, that's one less thing to explain. So prepare to explain away your inability to swim, the same way you have to explain that both your parents work fulltime and won't be able to pick you up and the same way you will have to explain why you don't take Monash brochures when university recruiters come around. You know you can't afford that.

A little way down the road, you may fool yourself into thinking that you belong here. You may get the accent right, attend the right events, speak to the right people but never lose sight of the real thing. The real thing being that sacrifices were made to get you to this place. Sacrifices by your parents to make sure you got way better opportunities than either of them ever did. Sacrifices to make sure that you never have to worry about things that they worried about. Sacrifices that when you walk into a room with your A school English, and your A school wokeness and your public income household work ethic and your public income household discipline, nobody can ever say no to you.

Because this is how your parents made you whole. They exposed you to every aspect of life so that you never again walk into a room and feel like you don't belong. They made you so you fit in everywhere and what a beautiful thing is that. To know there is not a conversation you can't have, or a narrative you can't be a part of.

But always remember, twice as hard, for half.

To Drunk Girls In Bathrooms

We call each other honey and babe and for the first time out of the many times we say that, we actually mean it. We hug each other and call each other pretty and help each other with toilet paper and lipgloss and we hold each other's hair when we throw up and we bitch about the stupid boys in our lives then we call each other pretty again, we hug and we never see each other again. See there's something special about drunk girls in a bathroom at 2am. It doesn't matter our differences out there, in here we are just a bunch of girls too wasted to notice these said differences.

I am tempted to highlight that here, in this room, where no boys are allowed, we thrive. We love each other, we support each other, and we get along. We don't stab each other in the back or call each other names or mean girl each other. We're a sisterhood here. I want to be naïve enough to say that we'll maintain this energy on Monday morning but who am I kidding?

On Monday morning, we're no longer the cute sisterhood we formed in the bathroom. On Monday morning, we are rivals. They have created a system where we have to fight each other for everything then they turn around and tell us it's not a competition. Oh but honeys it is. We want the same jobs, the same scholarships, the same opportunities, hell, we even want the same men, so don't let them tell you this isn't a competition.

And when this constant competing finally gets to us as it usually will, we'll always have our drunken encounters in the bathroom. How badly have we been pitted against each other that we have to be half way to insanity in order to get along? Whatever! So when we run into each other in the bathroom, drunk out of our minds, it's not a hug that we share. We are giving each other strength to make it through the following week. When we call each other cute, we are congratulating each other for having made it through another week.

And when we pull each other's hair back as we throw up, we're really saying. "I know you're tired. I am too. But this is the only way we get out of this alive." When we offer each other lip-gloss, we are really just saying, "Let them think they have won, let them have their victory dances because they don't have what we have". And what we have is each other at 2am, sloppy, clumsy but real. And here in this room where there are no boys allowed, we have never been stronger.

To Anyone Asking When I'll Get Married.

You sit TF down. I don't have time for this.

To My President

Look, this isn't a hashtag to get you off the presidential seat. We have tried the hashtag route way too many times and we know how that ends. With us disappointed and with you, back where you were. So no, this isn't that. Hashtags can only do so much and this is not part of the so much. So let's have an honest conversation. A conversation without big words like going and falling. Let's just have a chilled over coffee conversation between two citizens of the same country. Okay?

I think you owe a lot of people a lot of things. Perhaps this is why I'm not hell bent on giant notions like regime change. I need you to pay up what you owe before you can even think of going anywhere. See, people believe you when you talk. So when you say lives are going to improve, people expect their lives to improve. When you promise employment opportunities and better health care and a better education system, I don't think anyone is wrong to expect these to be delivered and I certainly don't think anyone is wrong to be angry when they feel like the delivery has failed.

Remember what I said about this being a very normal very everyday conversation between two people living in the same country? I think you are responsible for 14 million plus people and I think 14 million is a big number and I think that is something you need to be wary of. Every decision you make affects 14 million plus people and I don't think it's fair for any of these decisions to be taken lightly. 14 million plus! 14 million plus people who deserve better.

14 million plus people deserve critical thinking and application and opportunities, they need a fighting chance and right now, they don't have that. I'm not going to go into the details of how this fighting chance should come to be. That is not my place. It is instead the job you signed up for. Mine is to remind you of this number: 14 875 523

To Ota Benga

From the deepest parts of my heart, I am terribly sorry. Nothing I or anybody says can make up for what you went through. I keep trying to imagine what I would want someone to say to me if I had been through what you had been through but I come up with nothing. I hate that your name does not come up as much as it should. It should be up there with Emmett Till and Trayvon Martin but we are not here to compare tragedies.

I try to imagine how you must have felt being stuck in a literal cage with literal animals and it makes me sad. But more than that it makes me angry. How a teenage boy was reduced to a prop in some white man's game. The anxiety, the homesickness, the culture shock, again I can only imagine how you felt.

I am sorry. Nobody deserves to live or die the way you did. I wish I could tell you that your suffering was somehow worth it. This letter would be so much more powerful if I said you suffered so that black boys after you wouldn't have to. If I told you that the hell that you endured was so that none of your descendants would go through the same.

That would be a powerful letter. It would mean your sacrifice counted for something. Then I think about how disrespectful it is to use the word 'sacrifice". Sacrifices are voluntary; they are for a greater good. Yours was neither voluntary nor for the greater good. It was just another black casualty at the hands of a white man.

It wasn't a sacrifice. It was a statistic. I want so badly to say you died so black boys after you wouldn't have to. I want to say your fellow Africans were spared the humiliation of being a spectacle for the white man. But you died and that was it. Black people are still dying for no reason and there does not seem to be an end in sight. White people still come around here and oooh and ahhh at the way we live and take pictures of us at our worst then sell it off as art somewhere. So what was the point? Rest eternally beautiful black boy!

To Chimamanda Ngozi Adichie

I met you through my high school literature teacher and she had such nice things to say about you. I am ashamed to say that I fancied myself a reader and yet I did not know about your work at that point. Ever the eager student to please, I went home, found myself a copy of "Half of a Yellow Sun" and then I understood what my teacher loved.

Thank you for the gift of Kainene, who I think is the most badass woman in contemporary literature. You gave me a character that had so many layers to her, she was impossible to ignore. For the longest time, I had read about women who were either too good or just plain evil. Kainene was neither. In some of the best ways, she reminded me of myself. She had opinions, she was sure about them, she could hurt, she could be petty, she could be mean but she also had a heart so big, it extended to people who needed it. Perhaps I should have written her a letter too.

You are undoubtedly one of the most brilliant minds of our time and I consider myself lucky to have lived at a time when I was able to access your brilliance. Thank you for being an icon for black girls. Thank you for being an inspiration to African girls and for being a voice for black women everywhere. May we never forget what you gave to our generation.

Love and respect.

To Shonda Rhimes

In writing this letter I was going to tell you how much I want to be you. I was going to tell you how I have read your writings, watched your talks and speeches and watched your masterclasses and watched your interviews and how ever since I watched the Scandal pilot, I have been dreaming about becoming you. However, I recently watched one of your interviews and you said growing up, you wanted to be Toni Morrison. You mentioned that you later realised that you couldn't be Toni because Toni was being Toni and she wouldn't stop being Toni for a while. I then started to revise my own process. You're not going to leave your job soon and in all honesty, there can only be one Shonda Rhimes so I have learnt not to try to be you but to learn from you. So this is perhaps a thank you note to you.

Thank you for being proof that an introverted nerdy black girl can grow up and own television.

Thank you for reminding me to say yes. Yes to things that are scary, things that I would not otherwise do. Yes to playtime, a reminder that I should not take myself too seriously, that every now and then, I will need to unplug. Thank you for reminding me to say yes to difficult conversations, not to shy away from confrontation.

Above all, thank you for reminding me that nobody can do it all. The idea that when you're doing absolutely great in one aspect of your life, you are inevitably failing at another. For the longest time, I felt the pressure to be so good at everything that I did until you made me realise that it was impossible.

So while you read this, I'm ready to be hired. For whatever job, I will polish shoes, I will babysit, I will print copies, I will make a mean cup of coffee. Hell, I will follow you while you go about your day and I will shower you with compliments. (That sounded way less creepy in my head).

Thank you!

To Naya Rivera

It's the oddest thing to have to mourn someone that you didn't know personally. But I can't explain the many ways that your death touched me. I remember seeing on Facebook that you were missing and I thought someone had got something wrong because you had been so alive and so okay just a few hours before. And I remember the days following, I prayed hard that you would be brought back home. But even in my prayers, even when I kept the faith, a part of me knew that the worst was going to happen. Then the news came, I remember crying in my room, all while still trying to figure out how I could be so affected by someone I didn't know.

Then I remembered reading your book and how intimate it was and how honest it was. How could I not feel like I knew you when you poured your entire self into that book? And through it I got to know you for the person that you were. Honest. Witty. Mature beyond your years. And so hilarious even in situations where nobody expected humour. Now that you are gone and the tributes are pouring in, they only confirm what I already knew! They confirm that your heart was big and kind and could envelope anyone in love.

I keep thinking about the chapter in your book where you wrote about Cory Monteith's death. I go back to you calling Cory's death "unnecessary". Can't feel help the same way about yours. You were only 33 with so much to live for. You had a son you should have been able to see grow up, a family to care about, career goals to clear, and friends to be present for, love to give and even to get. This too feels unnecessary.

However, in good faith, I hope you found peace. You died a hero and in your final moments, you saved your baby. That is not a thing to mourn but a thing to respect and be in awe of. Rest Always Queen.

To Jada, You Were Wrong

I come in peace. I won't try to shame you for being "unfaithful" and I won't sympathize with Will for being "the victim". Whether or not you cheated is your business. You say you were separated. I believe you; you have no reason to lie. Even if you are lying, it's not my business. I am not here to disparage anybody as a wife or life partner of spouse or whatever. Again, it's not my business.

My issue is with a much larger conversation that a lot of people don't seem to be ready to have. My issue is with the borderline predatory behavior that you displayed. You said "...it all started with me wanting to help with his health and his mental state." I honestly kind of switched off after that because my issue was if you knew that this boy (at 22 or 23, you're just a boy, don't even try to argue with me) had mental issues, why was the next instinct to start a relationship with him? How is that the next logical step? Here is a person who is already vulnerable: he is physically sick, mentally he needs help, he has openly admitted to bouts of depression and suicidal thoughts and you a 40 something year old person who definitely knows better still decide to pursue a relationship with him. How?

Not only that you also said that you did it just to feel "good". Like I said, I'm not fighting with Jada the wife. I'm fighting with Jada the person. The fact that you knew that he was mentally and emotionally vulnerable and you still used him to "feel good", all under the guise of "helping him" is what doesn't sit right with me.

More so - your lack of accountability cripples me. You made this about your Jesus complex. "It was really a joy to help heal somebody- I think it has a lot to do with my co-dependency." Maam. Please. We all know somebody like this. Somebody who hides behind big words like "entanglement" and "co-dependency" and "interaction" just to run away from responsibility. And I strongly believe that is something you have mastered... weaponizing the healing process and the search for a better self and using it as ammunition.

I love you Jada. I have since I was a kid. But I also believe in accountability and you have shown none. With all of that being said, I admit that this really is none of my business. I'm just a bystander and giving a bystander's opinion. Ultimately, this has nothing to do with me.

To Amy Winehouse, P!NK and Halsey

You don't know me, although I don't entirely believe that. Your best work sounds like it was written straight from my heart. So maybe in a parallel universe you do know me. Maybe in that parallel universe, I send you (or ask you very politely) to deliver the kind of music that speaks to me in this universe.

You have filled a lot of my years with meaning and depth and on days when nothing seems to make sense I know I can always count on " Tears Dry on Their Own" or "Chaos and Piss" to be some level of order in a sea of chaos.

Your music has offered me comfort at the worst times, something to dance to in the good times and when boredom strikes, I know I always have something to go to for a session of karaoke or lip syncing.

Your words and voices have saved me from myself on so many instances. They are beautiful, they are true, they are honest. They are appreciated.

To Blair Waldorf.

I am 14 years old and looking for someone to look up to. I try a lot of icons but there is something wrong about each of them. Some are unreasonably pretty, some are unreasonably well disciplined, some unreasonably badly behaved, some are just too basic and then you walk in...

Blair Cornelia Waldorf in all her valor. Suddenly someone made sense to me and for me at 14 that was life changing. You showed a little girl that there was absolutely nothing wrong with knowing exactly what you want, even if it's at an early age. You taught me that it was okay to do to whatever it takes to get to where you want to be.

From you, I learnt that it is okay to be a little bad sometimes. It does not make you evil, it just makes you human. And you stayed human enough to care about family and friends and boys all in the middle of your journey to the top. I will always admire that.

I am 25 now and I am older than you ever were. Someone might say I'm even too old to be writing letters to a fictional character from a high school drama but you shaped a lot of who I became. You gave a little girl someone to aspire to be and someone to look up to. For years, I lived by the "What Would Blair Waldorf Do" rule and I think that should take credit for some of my victories.

I may be all grown up now but whenever I start to lose sight of what's really important, I still hear you in the back of my mind:

"If you really want something, you don't stop for anyone or anything until you get it."

To Chuck Bass

My childhood celebrity crush!

Three words. Eight letters. Say it and I'm all yours.

To Beth and Randall Pearson

Until I was 21, I had never seen an entirely functional black couple on TV. I had seen the Cosbys but that was comedy and knowing what we know now, that shouldn't be my point of reference. This has been said a hundred times over but it really is true: representation matters.

And until I saw you two, all I had to go on were the abusive black relationships that flood TV, laden with histories of abuse, prison and drug use. See, because there was so much of that in the media, in my head I figured that black love had to hurt.

I internalised a lot of that and even as I met guys and as I went into relationships, I didn't expect any of it to be all that good because I had never seen any of that reflected on TV. But then I saw you two and I realised that black love didn't have to hurt.

It could be easy and fun and comfortable and patient but above all, it could be healthy. A love healthy enough to let so much beauty grow around it and healthy enough to extend towards other people. You may not know it but that changed my outlook and my expectations of relationships.

So thank you for what you are doing for a whole community of people. You are showing that black fathers don't always have to be absent and black mothers aren't always yelling at somebody. You are proof that black husbands can be faithful and black wives aren't defined by being patient with years of bullshit.

Above all, thank you for giving a black girl a love to believe in and look forward to.

To Elena Gilbert

You maam are the most intolerable character I have ever seen on television and I absolutely hate you. I also would like to add that you are the reason why I stopped watching The Vampire Diaries. Listen, Elena, I sympathise with you. You caught a couple of tough breaks but geez, must you be so annoying? I was sold on the old Elena Gilbert charm on the first few episodes. Pretty girl, seemingly kind, everybody loves you but eventually it kind of got old.

The whole dating brothers thing will never not be weird. I get that in a world with vampires and witches and doppelgangers and werewolves, a sibling love triangle isn't all that scandalous but still. Also because you knew the complex history with Stefan and Damon and Katherine, you should not have put yourself in the middle of the brothers. Also those two were like a hundred years older than you and I am pretty sure there are actual laws against your relationship with both. Just makes this weirder.

I also still don't get your appeal. I hate how everybody was ready to sacrifice themselves to save you. Why? What is so special about Elena Gilbert? Let's do a quick rundown. Are you beautiful? Yes but that whole cast looks like it walked out of a magazine cover so we rule that out. Are you particularly fun person to hang out with? Again no, in eight seasons, the most fun I saw you have was getting red highlights in your hair. Jenna died to save you, John died to save you, Grams died because Bonnie was doing you a favour...what is the big deal here? Also the whole reason the series even started was because Stefan saw you and decided he "had to know you". What am I missing here? What is your appeal sis?

I am still to see a whinier person on TV. I hate how you made everything about yourself. And I hate how everybody else enabled your self-centredness and borderline narcissism. Remember when you thought Stefan could be saved from being the ripper by his love for you? And remember when you just went on a suicide mission with Damon for what reason exactly? I remember Damon driving into the grill to save the city from travellers...why were you there? I just have so many questions.

And your lack of accountability remains appalling to this day. You do remember your no humanity phase where you went on a blood sucking rampage, stole from Caroline, tried to kill Bonnie and actually killed a stranger? Yeah. You suck.

What kills me is that you had all the ingredients to be a decent human being but you became this, the absolute worst: just another annoying entitled white girl on TV.

Absolute love for Nina Dobrev but you...nah.

To Anyone Thinking of Writing A Book

Please do. As I wind down the writing of these letters, the only thing I can think of is "why didn't I think of this sooner?" There is so much story inside of you. You may not know it now but trust me once you sit down behind your desk and start aggressively poking at your keyboard, I promise, you will realise how much you have to tell. Tell it. Of course you will never be able to exhaust all of what you are thinking but what little you can, do.

The world is waiting for your voice. Although I should say, it isn't so much about the reception as it is about your process. You will love writing a book, you will hate it sometimes. It will tire you, it will scare you but I swear it will teach you more about yourself than anything has before. You will be a little uncertain at first but as you go further, the words will spill out of your heart and straight onto the page.

I can't wait to read it.

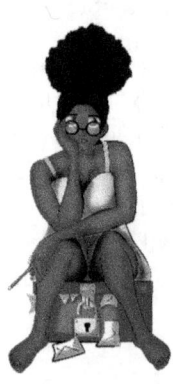

A MILLION LITTLE THINGS
"It has long been an axiom of mine that the little things are infinitely the most important."
— *Sir Arthur Conan Doyle*

To My Period

Bruh, just take it easy on me this month.

To Tampons

"You stay there and don't move an inch"

-Some guy on Titanic

To Privilege

The first time you rear your little head, I am four years old and it is my first day of preschool. I realise my teacher is an old white lady and I am elated. I almost feel relieved that I'm not in the class with the black teachers. I am four and I understand nothing about race but I am glad my teacher is white.

When I turn 9, you show up again. We are doing a religious skit and I terribly want to play Jesus Christ and I know no one will do it better. I am told Jesus can't be played by a girl. They say they will dress me up as a boy and have me play Simon Peter. I say if they can dress me up into Peter, they can surely dress me up into Christ. They say, "No, Christ was a leader." So I play Peter, Christ's cowardly loud mouthed sidekick.

Your next visit is when I am 13. My friend kisses a boy. He gets high fives and she gets called a slut. He is a hero, she is ignored. At 14, you let a boy call me ugly. I tell him where to you shove it. You allow him to say I am moody because I am on my period.

At 15, I watch you force my Muslim friend to read from the Christian Bible during school assembly because those are the rules of school. I watch her slowly egest the verse, word for word but I see it hurts her. This is not her God, these are not His words.

At 17, I watch you make my friend have to explain his sexuality to everybody he meets. He says he was born this way, they say he is a sinner. He tells them that it's not their place to say and they say his place is in hell.

I turn 19 and on my first day of college, you enable my lecturer to speak to me in a language I don't understand. I bring it to his attention and he continues talking. At 20, I tell my male friend that my lecturer is looking at me funny. My friend laughs and says now he knows why my grades are always this good.

I am 25 now and I am done explaining you to people. See, people are aware of you, privilege and for the longest time I thought they weren't. I would try to reason with people; explain how being male or rich or white or Christian or heterosexual or…whatever gave them an advantage over everybody else. I eventually realised that they were deliberately misunderstanding me. Deliberately ignoring your presence in their lives because acknowledging you meant they would have to start doing things differently.

I don't think anyone is ready for that.

To My Body

Listen, I know we've been at odds for about four or five years now but let's call a truce. In these four years, we have been so horrible to each other and I know that you've been through the most because of me but guess what; I've been through the most because of you too. I am still to understand how we got here, you and I had a great partnership for so long so I really don't understand why we are fighting right now but to call a truce, maybe we should start with a confrontation.

I hate how you casually just blow up like it doesn't mean anything. I get that you're not tiny and no one is asking you to be tiny but come on, you are also not this big. You have always been average sized and I don't get what this recent blow up is about. And I think your passive aggression is a little much. Don't think I don't notice how you never cared about pasta until I went on a diet then you decided to have the biggest pasta cravings, and those frost bites that you got when I tried using a cold compress to burn my your belly fat. That compress wasn't even that cold and the frost bite was a tad bit dramatic. I also feel like you're a bit of a wuss. Why can't you run the way other bodies do, remember those workouts I tried to commit to early this year, remember how you wouldn't jog because you were tired and you preferred power walking. I listened to you and I power walked and you were supposed to lose some weight, remember.

I am also ready to admit that maybe I don't take the best care of you. Maybe I could drink more water, or get more sun but is it really that bad? And maybe I neglect you sometimes or maybe I introduce you to far too many people but we're on the same team here. I bathe you, I feed you, I clothe you, I just need you to work with me here. And maybe I'm asking a lot by asking you to shrink yourself just for my benefit but I swear all I need you to do is try.

And if you try and fail- having tried then I will drop the weight thing. Then I will never speak of it. And I will love you, so unconditionally and so fiercely and I will love you in the way that you deserve to be loved. I just need to know that you tried.

To My Eating Disorder

Eight years into my eating disorder, my mother says to me "I hope this won't turn into Anorexia." I laugh it off and tell her not to worry. I tell her that nothing could ever come between me and my food. She believes it. We move on. I suppose she has noticed how I haven't had an actual meal in close to a week. She saw me pick a few grapes at breakfast and nap through lunch and say I wasn't hungry at supper.

Then I think back to the first time I realised something was wrong with my relationship with food. It must have been in 2013 and a boy I liked, liked somebody else. It seems silly now but I was 18 and that seemed like the end of the world. I remember eating a whole bunch of brownies in one sitting and when I finished, I remember feeling like crap. I also remember thinking that in the pool of crappy feelings; I would pick that crappiness over the crappiness of the boy not liking me.

That was the first step down a very slippery road. For years after that, I replaced confrontation with food, crying with food, feeling with food. What followed this substitution of human functions with food was a self-loathing that still brings me to tears. I hate myself after I've spent months eating. Naturally I blow up and then I get on the self-starving.

It's never that I don't want to eat. I do. But I think of whatever I eat building up in my body and adding up to this mess that I've already created. I remember once I spent the day on a strawberry and a couple of grapes and 3 bottles of water and that was it. I never talk about this to anybody because I don't look the way a person with an eating disorder looks.

I don't have any bones sticking out and I wouldn't appear on an episode of my 200 Pound life and so it doesn't make a lot of sense. I sound like a girl who doesn't want to be held accountable. But I need to have this talk with you, eating disorder:

I am done. I have given you so much power over my life, my restraint and my body for the longest time and I need to take all those back. And I understand that in a very twisted way you have been trying to help me. But I need to find other ways to be okay now. I can't do that with you around.

To My Anxiety

A lot of times, people have told me that they think I work hard. And I smile and I nod politely and I say thank you and I spin a line about work ethic and the value of hard work. Of course that's an easier line to dish out than to tell the truth. I would much rather tell people that I enjoy work than acknowledge you. Because let's face it, I work out of an irrational fear of disappointing than anything else. You are nearly the reason for everything I do and everything I don't.

I realise this is the first time I am acknowledging your existence. A lot of the time, I try to push you to the back of my mind and tell myself that I will deal with you eventually. Eventually can last a lifetime if you want it to and I've been putting this conversation off for years. I walk around you in the way I suppose people move around landmines, you move just an inch too close and everything just goes to shit. I can't do that forever.

I can't say for sure when you first came into my life but for as far back as I can think, I've grown to be so comfortable with you, I almost don't notice that you are an anomaly. I've carried you on my back for so long, I don't think I know myself outside of you.

Who am I if I'm no longer the girl who bit on her nails so hard, she started bleeding on her first day at an internship because she was so terrified she would screw everything up? Who am I if I am no longer the girl that stayed up, almost unable to breathe the night before an important interview? Or if I stop being the girl who just walks past people she knows so quickly because she is worried she will say the wrong thing? Or the girl who shows up well ahead of time because she gets literal palpitations at the mere thought of keeping somebody waiting.

I figure the most distinct parts of me are as a result of your presence in my life. Because of this, I'm a little reluctant to let you go. You're not all bad. I won't pretend you're a monster. You have pushed me to do some of my most amazing work and you have taught me to expect nothing less of myself. I appreciate that although I do feel that someday I will get to a place where I am able to produce results without you whispering in my ear the many ways it could go wrong.

I won't wish you away yet. Because like I said, who am I without you? You and I still have so much to do. Don't go just yet. I still don't know myself outside of you.

To My Inhaler

"How do I breaaaathe without you?

If you ever go,

How do I eveeeeeeeeeeer

 Ever survive? "

I'm sorry Leanne Rimes. This was way funnier in my head.

To My Glasses

An ode to you my second pair of eyes – without whom I would not be able to see or read or write or watch TV or type or function. Thank you. I'll admit, I was very sceptical when I first learnt I needed you. Having one of your primary functions start to decline at the age of 13 sucks majorly. Also needing glasses when you have eyes the size of mine feels like one of nature's most cruel jokes, But that's okay, I'm always good for a great joke.

Here we are, at the twelve year mark and I just want to extend my gratitude. Obviously I am thankful for the whole helping me see thing but you have done more than that. For years you have given people the impression that I am insanely smart. I will never understand that though – how people tend to think people in glasses are automatically smart. Glasses just mean we can't see but anyway. Thank you for giving off that illusion. It has served me well in a lot of situations.

I also want to thank you for keeping my introverted self well hidden behind your lenses. You do the Lord's work. You have been a great defence against conversations I didn't want to have, people I did not want to encounter and situations I did not want to be a part of. You are highly appreciated.

Side note: Don't think I don't notice how you've been unashamedly cock blocking me from the time that I started using you. Nobody sees a girl in glasses and thinks "Oh look, I'd like a piece of that" but that's okay. You give so much to me and if this is the price that I pay then I'm happy to. Overall, you've been a great sport and above all, I will never overlook that you are one of the longest commitments I have ever made.

To Chocolate and Cake

Darling, we need to stop meeting this way.

To The Gym

I'm sorry I gave up on you after just one day. I shouldn't have done that. It was only after I had given up on you that I realized that my thing with you wasn't a once off thing. I have a terrible habit of walking away from things too early. I will fix that. I will be back.

To My Size 32 Jeans

I hope you understand why I still keep you in my closet even though you no longer fit. It's just so hard to let you go. We've been together for so many years and the thought of discarding you breaks my heart. For the longest time, you were my perfect fit and now after all these years, to have to accept that we have come to the end of our road is a terrible pill to swallow. I guess I should finally gather the strength to do this.

See, you represent a time in my life when my body and I were in agreement. You remind me of a time when I could eat anything and get away with it. But let's be honest honey. I'm not 21 anymore. My choices of food don't go unpunished anymore. Everything shows and to be fair I have tried to stretch you out but you also aren't working with me. Anyway, as I was saying, I am in my mid 20s now and I cannot cheat the system anymore. This is what happens when you reach a certain age. Butts get bigger, hips get wider, bellies start seeping out of places they shouldn't be. At some point, size 32 jeans just stop fitting.

But I'll keep you - as a reminder of a time when all was well in the world. I'll always hold you dear to my heart and keep you safe in my closet. And I admit that I am keeping you under some misguided conception that I will one day work on my body to a point where I can fit into you once again. We both know that won't happen. So you will stay as a reminder. A beautiful reminder of a beauty that once was.

To The Hoodie I Refuse To Return

I know it's confusing. For years you belonged to him and then one day when it was cold he gave you to some girl who is your new owner now. Let's face, it wasn't even that cold that day and he just gave you away to make a statement, some sort of confirmation that he and I were solid. A hoodie will solidify any relationship. Why make a verbal commitment when you can just toss a hoodie, it's basically the same thing.

I guess you wonder why I keep you when I don't even wear you. I'm a very petty human being and I would rather keep you and not use you than let him have you back. He doesn't deserve to have you back. He deserves absolutely nothing. And now I just keep you as a consolation prize or some non-marital alimony. At the end of the mess box of a relationship, at least I get to keep a fucking hoodie. Lord knows I deserve more but I'll take the hoodie.

See, he and I had a pretty decent thing going and there was a time when I wore you proudly because you were a symbol. That I mattered to somebody, that I had a partner. And nothing gave me more joy than strutting around in you. I used to love how you smelled like him and whenever he was away, probably whoring himself off, I'd put you on and then it would feel like he was back here.

See, we're victims of the same selfish man child. A guy who never realises the value of what he has. You're a good hoodie and I'm a good girl and he gave up on both of us. Doesn't it bother you how easily he discarded you and just gave you up? Then you probably started to wonder where the problem was. Were you not warm enough or cute enough or black enough? Oh but honey you were. He was the problem.

So you get why I can't return you. He doesn't get to have you back. You don't exist at his beck and call. We are so alike, you and me. Call us the sisterhood of the discarded. So let this be our rebellion. Let's band together and stay here. Away from him. And as day turns to night, and help feels colder and colder, let him remember, he should not have been so quick to let us go.

To Vodka

You have carried me through some of my darkest times.

You have been the reason behind some of my best memories.

You have motivated some of my worst decisions.

But you have been incredibly loyal.

I thank you.

Should I evolve to a point where I no longer need you, I will miss you terribly.

To My Bedroom

I apologise for the constant mess I keep you in but I'm sure by now you understand that in the middle of that chaos there is a pattern that only you and I understand. You have been my home, my office, my solace, my bunker, my naughty corner for the longest time and you are still as safe now as you were when I was just a little girl. Your consistency is noted and not overlooked. Not even for the slightest second.

You held me calm when I got my first period and started googling haemorrhage. Not once did you call me dramatic, it was just menstruation. When I started whispering to boys on the phone, you kept your walls thick enough that my parents in the next room never heard a word. You kept your lights on through a hundred nights of study and chasing deadlines and thinking up ideas and you okayed all of them, big and small and good and bad.

You hugged me in the nights that I cried and you let my tears soak into you as you soothed words of comfort and words of "It gets better" and "You are never alone" even though most of my lowest moments were just witnessed by me and you. When I knelt on your floors to pray, you let me. Never being so hard that I felt the need to get up before I was finished. When I wanted to look pretty, your mirrors looked back with encouragements of "You don't need all that makeup" but still smiled back when I did put on all that make up.

As I grow older, I am fonder of you now than I ever was then but at the back of my mind, there is always that sense of impending doom. That one day I will leave you and never come back. That all our secrets, and victories and losses won't be ours anymore. They will be mine because I lived them and yours because you witnessed them but never fully ours again.

To Boarding School

I am not ashamed to say that for a little bit, I hated my parents for deciding we should meet. However, I guess I should thank you now. It didn't feel like it when we were together but I suppose you were preparing me for adult life. Independence away from home, thick skin so that no one anywhere in the world can try to walk all over me, self-sufficiency when resources run out. You also taught me that all the entertainment I needed was within me and because of that I can never get bored.

Most importantly you introduced me to some of the most amazing people that I know I can count on-even 12 years later. I guess that was the point- that I get a network of people who watched me- who I watched grow as well. I know all I did when we were together was complain but I get it now. I would not be the person I am today if it hadn't been for you.

P.S: I get that all these things were meant to make me a better person but what did the cold winter baths have to do with anything?

To My University Degree

Took a whole four years but we finally did it. You are to date the most responsible thing I have ever done and for that you will always hold a special place in my heart. You're the one thing no one can ever take away from me and your loyalty is highly appreciated.

More than a lot of things, you taught me perseverance. You taught me that eight hours of sleep are overrated and you taught me that the human body can function fully on noodles, tinned fish and no water at all. You taught me resilience, patience and the whole falling 99 times and getting up a hundred times bit. I stumbled across a lot of things to finally get to you, you beauty.

I survived ethnic micro-aggressions, alcohol, drugs, break ups, make ups and fights just to get to you and that makes you all the more impressive. Thank you for helping me grow up. Four years away from home will do that. But I will always be grateful for the many people that you introduced me to. It was through you that I met some of the best people. We spent days and nights talking, laughing and being outright stupid with no idea that we were living through some of the best days of our lives. These people became my lifelong friends- people I know will always have my back.

You also led me to friends who always had advice to give, roommates who always had the best gossip, lecturers who were sometimes insightful and sometimes sadly underwhelming and classmates who always tested my patience. Thank you for each of them.

None of that matters now though. I have you. And I am so proud of you. I promise you will not be forgotten. I will make it a point to very subtly sneak you into conversation. I also promise that you will not be alone forever. I promise that I will get one or two more of you because you deserve the company. But even then, you will always be special because you will always be my first.

To The 5+ Years Missing From Zimbabwean History

My father was not the kind of man who cried but once when I asked him what his 20s were like, tears formed in his tears as he recounted how he couldn't travel to see his family for three years. He said men like him couldn't just travel to their home villages because men like him were being hunted down and being called criminals and dissidents and ugly words like that. He said men like him were being hunted down by men who looked like him but just didn't talk like him.

An elderly relative of mine died last year. The pastor said she died peacefully in her sleep. Oh but I know there was nothing peaceful about her sleep. She hadn't slept a full night since the winter of 85 when she slept and woke up to find one of her sons missing. Perhaps in heaven, if heaven has the answers, she may be able to rest. I think about the son that she lost. I'm told he was a very simple boy. He stayed in his lane, didn't interfere with protocol; his simple mind could never conjure up any of what he was accused of. All he wanted to do was wake up one morning and be the deadbeat that he had always been. None of which was a crime.

I replay all these scenarios in my head and I think about how we tiptoe around them when we have "national conversations". How we call genocide and wiping out of entire ethnicities of people "a moment of madness". Leaving your cooking spoon in the fridge and forgetting it there is a moment of madness, plugging your phone onto the charger and not turning the power on is a moment of madness. Going on a five year rampage of killing people is not a moment of madness, it is cruelty.

I just want an admission. And admission that there isn't much of a difference between the people behind this cruelty and the white man that the same people allegedly fought. An admission of how fellow black men were killed for no other reason than the language they spoke. You know the enthusiasm that we have for talking about the evils of the white man; I want the same enthusiasm when talking about how huts were burnt down with living people inside.

I want to know how people can ride on their high horses come back to the places where these atrocities were done and try to preach peace. Preaching peace as they walk over the bones of sons and brothers and uncles and fathers. Standing over them as if they don't feel the weight of their blood on the soles of their shoes.

See, when people put up hashtags and gather resources to #bring back people and #free other people, I sympathise, I swear I do. But I also want a hashtag for the many people whose names we will never know, people who never got to be what they wanted to be but more importantly, people who we spent years pretending didn't die the way they did.

To the Year 2019

First off let me say that none of what you did was funny. Second, I've been around for 24 years and you've only been at this for 365 days and there's no way you could have won this one. You lose, I win-let's move on.

I may never forgive you for taking my dad away from me and sending me into the most confused, most confusing 7 months of my life. I won't forgive you for everything that he would have been so proud of that he'll never get to be and the panic attacks that I'm so tired of concealing. I won't forgive you for the month I spent locked up at home with no idea what I was doing and I may never forgive you for the time I cried every night for 43 days straight. What I'll definitely not forgive you for is how I sometimes don't know what to say to God anymore. What do I say? Where do I start?

I hate what you did to my mother. No one with that much joy should ever go through that much pain. She's doing just fine by the way. I also hate what you did to my sister. The kid loves her job-probably even more than she loves me. But she quit-walked away and never looked back coz of all the nonsense you put her through. The silence through the phone every time I call my brother is also on you. There's so much to say yet so little. Again...What do I say? Where do I start?

On the flip side, there are things I've learnt about myself. Granted I could have learned them with the benefit of a parent but okay. I said earlier that I may never forgive you but maybe I will. Not because you earned it but because I deserve it. I deserve to walk away from this crap pool that you've dragged me into. So I'm leaving you behind. You and your grief and pain and self-doubt and...also you suck very much sir (I don't know but in my head you are a man) and I need to remove myself from the situation. Like I said, you lose, I win.

To Covid 19

I learnt today that you are what is called Force Majeure. Something that some might even go so far as to call an act of God. So I respect you, as an act of God. I won't be cursing at you or any of that. An act of God needs to treated as one.

So respectfully, let's get the awkwardness out of the way. I feel a certain way about you for disrupting my life the way you did. I don't think it's funny how you just pooped over my plans to have my second graduation before I turned 25. These are just little things I suppose. And it's quite selfish of me to obsess over this as if I am the only person who has been affected by your presence.

I think of people in healthcare who have to face you every day and try to fight you off other people, all while trying to fight you off themselves and I can't imagine what they are going through. I think of people with relatives who have had to live with you, people who can't see their relatives despite them needing them now more than most times. I also think of people who have lost their lives because of you and I know how selfish and entitled it is of me to be complaining about a delayed achievement.

While we're treating you as an act of God, I need to find the silver lining here. All acts of God come with a hidden silver lining and I suppose yours is this. Perhaps you are here to remind us of what really matters. You exist to remind us that life isn't promised and that we shouldn't take anything for granted. To appreciate every opportunity we get to go out and meet loved ones, to never take for granted the clean air that we breathe, the hugs that we give people, the ability to gather for a wedding.

I'll take you as a moment of introspection, an opportunity to get to learn myself. When was the last time anyone ever really had any time to learn about themselves? To discover what they loved and wanted out of life? Now is that time I suppose, hell its even the time to start writing that book that I always wanted to. So that's what I will do.

No act of God is a mistake. And I believe you are no different. This I suppose is all part of a grander plan that in the grandest scheme of things, we will all come to acknowledge that you were good for something.

www.ingramcontent.com/pod-product-compliance
Lightning Source LLC
LaVergne TN
LVHW011708060526
838200LV00051B/2806